Romantic Country Style

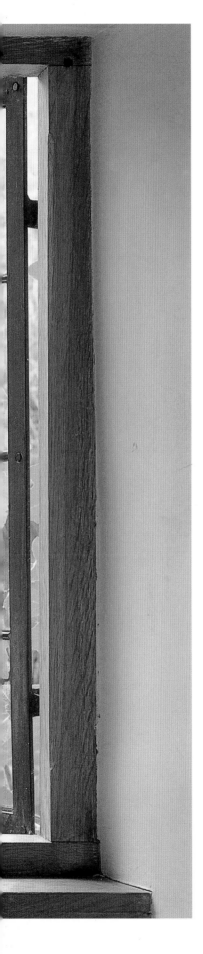

From the Editors of Victoria *Magazine*

Romantic Country Style

Text by Judy Spours

HEARST BOOKS

A Division of Sterling Publishing Co., Inc.

NEW YORK

Book Design by Christine Wood

Library of Congress Cataloging-in-Publication Data
Available upon request.

10 9 8 7 6 5 4 3 2 1

First Paperback Edition 2003
Published by Hearst Books
A Division of Sterling Publishing Co., Inc.
387 Park Avenue South, New York, NY 10016

Victoria is a trademark owned by Hearst Magazines Property, Inc., in USA,
and Hearst Communications, Inc., in Canada. Hearst Books is a trademark of
Hearst Communications, Inc.

www.victoriamag.com

Distributed in Canada by Sterling Publishing
c/o Canadian Manda Group, One Atlantic Avenue, Suite 105
Toronto, Ontario, Canada M6K 3E7

Distributed in Australia by Capricorn Link (Australia) Pty. Ltd.
P.O. Box 704, Windsor, NSW 2756 Australia

Printed in China

ISBN 1-58816-234-6

CONTENTS

FOREWORD

We all live in busy times. Computers command our lives at work; at home, we now connect to a world wide web for information and to keep in touch with friends and family. A new century and a new millenium are at our doorsteps. When we take the temperature of the world around us it is rising all the time with demands on us we never imagined. Amidst all this, nothing appeals to us more than a home with comfort and serenity, filled with the things we love, filled with reassurance that no matter how much things change, there is always home to come home to.

In this book we celebrate the romantic English country style that so many of us love for it is a personal expression of how we wish to live. Room by room this book becomes a guide to help you create surroundings that are charming, warm, engaging, and most of all, personal. There is no formula for a romantic life style. But there is a direction, and that is what our pages will show. Combine a mellow fabric with a wood finish that looks timeless, even if it's really not, and you are on the way to giving yourself a home where stress is not an invited guest.

All of us adore what romantic country implies – mostly a friendliness that brings us the notion that sunny days are celebrated and rainy days have their purpose as well. Be cozy in your home, be happy among the charming and enduring, and most of all, be comfortable.

So begin a new romance with home here. You do not have to have a beamed cottage in Devon or Sussex to take your tea and write your letters in an environment that goes back to a land where such simple pleasures are still honored. Home is an art, and with this book, we hope you can make your home the haven these century-old cottages have always been.

NANCY LINDEMEYER
Founding Editor,
Victoria Magazine

INTRODUCTION

T HE ENDURING APPEAL OF THE COUNTRYSIDE draws more and
more people every year. Some manage to fulfil their dream of
living and working there, while many more visit for weekends
and vacations, to relax and breathe in the fresh air before returning,
restored, to town or city.

The rural idyll conjures up images of beauty, tranquility, a closeness to
nature. With our increasingly busy lives, there is little time to stand back
and appreciate the changing of the seasons and the traditional values that
gave meaning to a bygone age. But while it may not be possible for us to
move to the country, and regain what has been lost, we can quite easily
introduce some of its desirable themes into our immediate surroundings,
wherever we live.

This is the reason why the country decorating style is so attractive and
remains ever-popular. It is achievable by everyone. It is not dictated by
changing fashion trends and there are no strict rules to be followed. It has

A kitchen corner spells country style clearly and brightly. The wood paneling is painted in a cheerful grass green; earthenware pitchers are used for utensils and for old-fashioned roses cut from the garden; and a stencil painted on the tiles above the practical, rectangular sink depicts domestic cattle.

evolved slowly over the centuries and continues to do so, refined and adapted according to practical and decorative considerations. Its great advantage is that it is supremely adaptable and can work equally well in a small apartment in the center of a city and in a large country house. The overall aim of this style is to create a haven where you can retreat, rest and entertain.

Colors, textures, and materials in the country home are natural; styles are understated, comfortable and informal; decorations are eclectic. The look at its best is in sympathy with the environment, relaxing into it rather than standing out from it. As the photographs in the following chapters demonstrate, country style also incorporates furnishing and decorating ideas drawn from different countries that can enrich our own culture.

In addition, contemporary country style is about an undemanding mix of old and new. The history and original appearance of an interior should be apparent, but its look may also include new furnishings arranged alongside. The old is not discarded, but nature is about renewal, not nostalgia. Neither does it mean we must forgo the modern comforts of efficient heating and glazing technology that we now almost take for granted, as they can now blend in almost seamlessly.

The country style is accessible when we keep to the fore the concerns that have influenced decorators past and present. The central principles soon become apparent: practicality, simplicity, harmony with nature, and a gradual, organic development. These ideals may seem a long way from the basics of colour swatches and paintbrushes, but they can in fact act as a invaluable template for the country decorating style.

This is breakfast in the country: piles of buttred wholewheat toast and waiting for a spoonful of local honey. A plain gingham tablecloth is decorated with a jar of wild flowers.

INGREDIENTS

Simple, spare, and informal

Romantic country style is a way of life

AKE ONE COUNTRY HOME and gently
blend in all the practical elements needed
for everyday life. Crack open a paint box,
mix well and add color. Flavor the mixture with
fabrics and decorative bric-a-brac and, finally,
sprinkle in the spice of life! Leave to mellow for a
few years, and enjoy.

The ingredients that make up a country style
depend on many factors – the architecture of the
home, the location, the lifestyle and tastes of its
owners, for example – but in this first chapter, three
important areas are discussed as a starting point
when thinking about the look and decoration of the
home. The first is an assessment of the innate
characteristics of country style, which are identified
here as a way of thinking and seeing rather than as a
checklist of items that must be obtained. The second
is a down-to-earth review of the use of color, the
aspect of decorating that is uniquely exciting and
daunting at one and the same time. The third is
fabrics, because the character of country interiors is
so closely identified with an idiosyncratic mix of soft
furnishing materials.

This introductory chapter is not without specific
inspiration, as the pictures illustrate rooms and
decorative details from a wide range of wonderful
country homes. The pictures alone serve as a visual
scrapbook, particularly in the "Get the Look" pages
in this chapter and throughout the book, which give
snippets of colors, furniture, and furnishings, along
with practical and decorative objects, any of which
may stick in the mind and prove a useful source of
inspiration when decorating.

Above all, this first chapter is an invitation to be
relaxed about country style and decoration, to get
into an unhurried mood that will, paradoxically,
eventually bring about the best results.

ABOVE *Form follows function in a country kitchen. Here a jelly cabinet
protects the food from insects, and a collection of wooden spoons is close
at hand, ready for use.*

RIGHT *Blue-and-white china, from all eras and styles, is what we
expect to see on the shelves of a country dresser. Here the pieces have
been chosen for their individuality, not because each is in a perfect
state of repair.*

Red, yellow, and blue – the primary colors – are here diluted, washed, or softened so that they appear suitably gentle and textured on country walls. The colors are bright and lively, but they are not domineering. They fit into the wider scheme of the overall decoration of a room, and they enhance the architecture rather than obliterating it.

Tiles are eminently suited to country interiors because they are chosen first and foremost for their practicality. They are hard-wearing and easy to clean; they are used on walls, floors, and work surfaces, and they last for years Tiles are also decorative, with deep, glazed-in colors and painted or embossed like the Victorian examples pictured here.

Let the light shine in and that fresh country air blow freely! Every window opportunity is exploited here – a large bay, an attic roof window, a wonderful barn with a glass wall, and

a tiny aperture that looks as though it was designed to be used by an archer. The view out, to the wider landscape, is as important as the light coming in.

The simplest way in which to combine the colors, patterns, and textures of fabrics is by stitching them together as patchwork. They can be designed in sophisticated, planned patterns,

or household scraps can be used randomly. Even very contrasting pieces of materials will mellow with age and look as though they were always meant to be together.

ESSENTIAL ELEMENTS

The essential elements of country style today are found in aspects of a way of living rather than in a list of objects and decorative schemes that must be in place in order to achieve the look.

Practicality is the starting point. Objects that work with their surroundings and for the convenience of the people using them have their own special beauty; it is this quality that attracts us to rural styles in the first place. The simple cottage interior appears comforting and integral to the people who live and work there. Furnishings are chosen for their hard-working characteristics, and they take on a particular aesthetic through years of honest service. A basic wooden settle, for example, is sturdy enough for constant use, cannot be easily damaged, and looks beautiful simply with generations of waxing of its irregularities. The country style today cries out for furniture to be selected for similar reasons, rather than because it is the latest designer piece.

LEFT *Natural materials mix together successfully: honest old wood, battered ironwork and tin, basketwork, and old linen lace. A flower arrangement of foxgloves, bracken, and grasses in a plain white pitcher epitomizes the simple country look.*

BELOW *The beauty of white on white is striking in the corner of this bathroom. Treasures from the natural world – feathers, a shell, a smooth pebble – are brought inside as decorations.*

To achieve the very best in design, choose the style of your furnishings and decorative elements with their function clearly in mind. Design professionals encourage people to view decorative objects in this light. They often believe that it is essential for there to be an honesty inherent in the design of everyday objects, particularly those that are mass-produced. Good design is found in a piece that is right for the job, responds fully to the functions for which it is intended, and is not too elaborate. A piece that may first be pleasing to look at is, in their eyes, dishonest, and is of no use if it doesn't work properly. For example, there is no point in a chair being good to look at if it is uncomfortable to sit in or difficult to get out of once you are seated.

Many country dwellers of recent years have been keen to adopt these ideas, to return to design basics as they try to take a more down-to-earth approach to life. They are keen, too, for the decoration of their houses to be in harmony with the natural world. This brings us to the next important element of country style, the use of natural materials and colors. The interior decorations are characterized by the use of stone and wood, wool and cotton, earth tones and neutral colors, which are in keeping with the outdoors environment visible through the doors and windows. Synthetic materials and unnatural-looking colors do not sit easily in a rural environment. If the walls of the house are painted in acid tones and the tablecloths made from shiny, brightly colored plastics, the home will look as though it has been dropped into the countryside from another planet. This choice of materials extends right down to the smallest objects in the home, such as wooden spoons stored in an earthenware pot in the kitchen, or a natural sponge sitting by the side of the bathtub.

An essential element of the style – again, a concept rather than a decorating dictate – is growth. Country style develops over time; it is not a look that can be instantly imposed upon a home. Very few of us are able to think of everything we need for the home and then find it all immediately – we must have time to consider what we need, where we should put it, and what it should look like. A room interior that grows organically and has elements added over the months and years will develop a decorative personality, reflecting the individuality of its owner. It will have an uncontrived charm that is usually lacking in an instantaneous scheme.

The natural world outside is intimately involved with the life and look of the country home. Doors remain open to the garden, and items from nature's decorative repertoire enter the house, perhaps by way of a

Is this house or garden? The two worlds

meet in this corner of a country home.

Earthenware pots and a wonderful
collection of baskets are ready to be filled
with market produce. The walls are
unpainted and the dresser scrubbed bare,
but this scullery corner has its own
decorative appeal.

collection of pebbles on a plate, pieces of driftwood decorating a windowsill, or simply vases of wild flowers and berries. Conversely, elements from inside the home find their way out of doors. Chairs and tables are set on the lawn, pieces of sculpture may be placed in the undergrowth of a flower-bed, and carefully positioned electric lights can make the garden a mystical gallery after dark. In this way, a relationship between the home and its setting is established, and it is one that is central to country style.

COLOR IN DECORATION

Country home decorators who are considering choices of color have a great advantage over their urban cousins because nature, the world's greatest colorist, is right outside the door.

Nature is relaxed about colors. There is no great debate about whether this goes with that, whether blue and green can be seen together, or whether yellow and orange are too bright a combination. Nature just throws them all together, boldly and without inhibition, and it looks good regardless. Nature also takes things slowly, perhaps starting with a backdrop of green in the foliage of trees and shrubs and grass, and waiting awhile before the plants mature, flower, and introduce additional colors to the scheme. Color accents are all-important. The natural scene may look harmonious but perhaps a little dull, then suddenly a few self-seeded red or yellow poppies burst open. Or, after a cold and frosty night, a bare winter scene is transformed with orange berries.

When asked about our favorite color, most of us can answer immediately, but our strong preferences seem to desert us when it comes to choosing colors to decorate the home. It is as though we know, or think we know, too much. We've learned that this or that color will create a particular mood, or make a room warm or chilly; and that one color is considered tasteful while another is not. There are concerns about which colors are deemed to "go together" and which are not, what constitutes a good contrast and what is a clash. There are also some aspects of color theory that we feel we should understand. And then there is fashion – the monster that influences us all in subtle ways and, quite maddeningly, can actually prevent us from finding the colors we want in the materials available at a particular time.

ABOVE *In this brave scheme, warm, bright colors – scarlet, yellow, and gold – are cunningly combined with pale turquoise and rich blue, which accentuate the look and prevent it from becoming claustrophobic.*

RIGHT *The colors used in a hall and in the kitchen beyond are varied but within the same gray/pastel tonal range. As a result, they sit together comfortably.*

Although we cannot hope to achieve anything like nature's level of color expertise, we can certainly learn from it and gain a little more confidence. So, first, consider the importance of a relaxed approach. Try ignoring all the information and worries you have about color and simply go for what you like. This approach can be enormously liberating and will give you the best possible chance of getting it right. If certain colors go together in your mind's eye and are pleasing enough for you to like them so much, why wouldn't they look good in a room scheme?

Second, exercise a bit of courage in your choice. Being daring in the use of color in interior decoration is difficult, but always worth the trouble and angst. The biggest mistake is to come up with the decorating colors you really want and think would look fantastic and then water them down until the original idea is lost and you are left with a spiritless compromise. The fear that leads to this situation is that we will spend a lot on something dramatic but not versatile and that it will prove an expensive mistake. However, the largest expenditure is on furniture, draperies, and carpets, not on paint. Therefore, if you prefer, play it safe with the more expensive furnishings but be brave in your choice of color for the walls. If the worst comes to the worst, correcting the mistake will entail only the price of a few cans of paint.

This leads on to the next lesson, the need to take things slowly. Don't rush out and buy a pretty collection of colored pillows and throws, and then try to match the vast areas of wall, ceiling, and floor around them. Like nature, go for the backdrop first: paint or paper the walls and then get plenty of large samples of fabrics and other furnishings to see what looks good with the background color. Remember, the room does not have to look perfect within weeks. The evolving,

The deep, polished colors of the antique wooden furniture in this dining room are allowed to take precedence over the decoration. The white walls and dull green staircase and beams are also a fine background for the paintings, which cry out to be examined individually.

ever-growing country style provides the perfect excuse to do things at a steady pace, adding color elements one at a time and living with them for a while before moving on to incorporate the next.

Finally, there are the fun accents that bring a color scheme alive. Even when the colors of the walls, floors, drapery fabrics, and woodwork tone beautifully and subtly, the overall effect may still not quite work. Then a chair upholstered in a completely different color is introduced, creating a visual tension in the room, and suddenly everything comes to life. This is the time, not before, to choose the pillows or other accents to fulfill this role.

Once your approach to color becomes free-spirited and confident, inspired by the workings of nature, you are ready to learn a little color

LEFT *The earthy, neutral shades of this corner of a country living room are brought alive by the simplest device: a silver vase of white lilies.*

RIGHT *"Blue and green should never be seen..." Forget the old adage; this room shows what a lively atmosphere the two colors can create in clever juxtaposition.*

theory. There are three basics to be aware of when dealing with color in decoration: tone, texture, and light.

There is no secret to tone in color. Tones are created by adding black or white to a hue. A tonal range is best described by example. Imagine a selection of different colors derived from natural pigments: it may include orange, cobalt blue, spice yellow, and olive green. Although the colors are different, their feel is similar – they appear to have the same intensity, the same shading. Now, imagine putting them next to an artificial green marker pen. It doesn't go, as the nature of the color is different from that of the natural pigments: it is from a different tonal range. Tone is something the eye can judge quickly, and as a general rule, colors from the same tonal range will look fine together (although the danger is they can look a touch bland), whereas colors in differing tones will clash and not look good. This is true even if the two colors are themselves similar: the spice yellow goes better with the olive green than the artificial green does with the olive.

Colors look different depending on the texture of the materials they consist of. Thus, orange high-gloss paint will have a different appearance to orange-tinted limewash. You can play with a limited palette of colors combined with a variety of textures; or, vice versa, a large range of colors all in the same texture.

Light is the final part of the color scheme. We all know that a surface absorbs or reflects light which we then perceive as a particular color. As a result, colors look

LEFT *The effect that light has upon color is evident in this tightly packed cottage where some corners are bathed in sunlight and others have almost no natural light at all.*

RIGHT *The use of only two colors – dark red and apple green – could be boring, but the mix of textures and patterns here makes the effect engaging.*

LEFT *Nature, the inspired colorist, went to work on rich golden shades that she sculpted into tufts of plumage for this handsome rooster.*

BELOW *The rose has it all: colors subtly shaded from one tone to another, and the inimitable texture of the petals.*

BELOW RIGHT *Fall is the season above all others when we notice the brilliance of nature's color combinations. A tonal range could not be better exemplified than in the changing shades of leaves and fruit as the season progresses.*

different according to the amount and quality of the light. You need to look at them in both the available daylight of the room and the artificial light you will be using after dark, and consider the implications. If the room is a kitchen used throughout the day, the way it looks in daylight is paramount; if it is a dining room used mostly in the evenings, the color effects with electric and candle light dictate your choice.

Color is an enormous joy, and our preferences are very personal. We cannot know whether our perception of a particular color is the same as someone else's. Perhaps it is not, which might explain individual preferences. Go for what you like, for the colors that stimulate your own eye.

FABRICS

The two characteristics of country fabrics that immediately spring to mind are informal pattern and natural yarns, predominantly cottons. Rich velvets and chenilles, formal stripes, and large repeating patterns are the stuff of urban fabrics and would look out of place in the country, except in a very grand country house. For many people, the quintessential country fabric is a faded chintz, a printed cotton decorated with pale roses and other herbaceous plants.

The word "chintz," which derives from the Hindi *chint*, was originally used to describe painted calicoes imported into the West from the Indian subcontinent. By the seventeenth century, printed cottons in many colors and intricate patterns from the East took Europe by storm. Importers such as the East India Companies did huge trade in the fabrics, even persuading Indian manufacturers to use European motifs. By the eighteenth century, European manufacturers began to compete by producing their own printed cottons. The vogue for floral designs gradually developed and the name chintz came to be used to describe these familiar flower-printed cottons. Today, the name refers to any glazed cotton material used for furnishing, whether patterned or plain.

By the early twentieth century, chintz was synonymous with English country house style, and the majority depicted garden flowers such as roses, carnations, and peonies. Some concentrated on tree foliage, while others harked back to the pictorial designs of earlier centuries and featured garden ornaments such as sundials and birdbaths, or ribbons and swags. These are the designs that link the interior design of the country home with its garden. The natural world is used in motif, a constant reminder of the beauties of nature.

Chintz fabrics have been used all over the country house, in sitting rooms, dining rooms, and bedrooms, and they are still enormously popular. Today, we favour faded chintzes in muted shades – quite different from the originals – because they give an instant impression of antiquity and lived-in comfort. As a result, contemporary manufacturers produce "pre-faded" chintz patterns that are new but resemble antique textiles. In recent years, some fabrics have been modernized versions of chintz, with flowers spaced out at intervals across a solid color background. The patterns have stronger outlines and are less tightly packed than the earlier floral designs, but they are well within the same tradition.

The greatest single influence brought to bear on British rural fabrics was that of the designs of William Morris and his company, who

An old chintz comforter, edged in brilliant orange, goes well with the bright spice colors of an Indian-inspired printed cotton.

RIGHT *A homage to red, white, and blue fabrics is found here – in gingham, large checks, stripes, toile de Jouy, and quilts.*

FAR RIGHT *A modern linen cupboard displays fashionable fabrics in indigo blue and white: stripes reminiscent of ticking for pillows and bolsters, and tie-dyed Indian throws.*

BELOW *Simple rural cottons, printed with traditional dye colors, blow in the wind in an apple orchard.*

produced hand-blocked linens and cottons, together with tapestries and carpets, from the 1870s. The designs featured flowers and plants, such as tulips and marigolds, that were more stylized and exotic than the species depicted in conventional chintzes, and often incorporated birds and other animals. A number are still mass-produced today in both original and new colorways and remain extremely popular. Many a country home will have a room decorated with willow-pattern or honeysuckle-printed curtains designed by Morris over a century ago.

Checks, particularly the one-color ginghams, are also closely associated with the country home style. The crisp simplicity of gingham – usually in dark blue, dark green, red, or yellow with white – is deeply resonant of a simpler way of life, when everything from kitchen curtains to little girls' summer dresses seemed to be sewn from gingham checks. This nostalgia, coupled with the inherent simplicity of its design, has guaranteed the continuing popularity of the fabric, which is used both in informal country rooms and in grand interior design schemes. Ginghams are used for tablecloths, curtains, shades, slipcovers, pillows, bedspreads, quilts, dust ruffles – virtually all the decorator fabrics in the home.

Country home style in fabrics is often achieved with a lively mixture of these variously patterned materials. A living room, for example, may contain floral chintz slipcovers alongside ginghams and other checks, often with original Eastern designs thrown in. The look can be successful when it is very simple, with a few faded old armchairs and the odd Indian throw; or it can be quite grand, as in the designs of the interior designers who have interpreted the style to produce a look reminiscent of elegant eighteenth-century society living.

The developing fashion for simpler interior design, associated with a return to a more basic and "honest" way of living, has resulted in plain, unadorned fabrics becoming popular. Undyed natural linens, bleached cottons, and utilitarian fabrics such as striped mattress ticking and other lining materials are now on unashamed display in country interiors designed along principles of simplicity. At its best, such a use of fabrics allows the interior architecture of old buildings to shine through the furnishings and be enjoyed for its own sake. This look has more to do with texture than with color or pattern, which is why the fabrics fit in so well. The texture and materials of old walls and wooden beams, stone floors and fireplaces are complemented by the prominent weaves of heavy woven draperies and upholstery.

It is an appealing style, but not one with a particularly strong historical basis. Our country ancestors would never have dreamed of using linen dish towels to make curtains or shades as some country home owners do today; this would have signaled

The inspiration for classic chintz: a glorious summer flower garden.

poverty and would have been avoided at all costs. As in all other spheres, the basics alone lose their appeal if you can afford nothing more.

Similarly, there has been a revival of rag-rugs, which are now mass-produced as part of the style, but were once painstakingly made out of old scraps by the thrifty rural housewife. A couple of centuries ago, if the household was really poor, the housewife would have thrown down old burlap to add a semblance of comfort to the hearthside. Even this look has been appropriated in the taste for sisal and coir matting in contemporary interiors.

Lilac-tree chintz and simple sprigged cottons are used to great effect on pillows in an otherwise plain interior.

Inexpensive oriental cottons remain in vogue in England – anything from traditional Indian prints to translucent, one-color muslins. Nowadays they are sometimes found mixed with other Eastern fabrics, such as tie-dyed patterns (originating in India) or batik (an art that reached its apotheosis in Java).

The country home bedroom still has its starched linen sheets, lace coverlets and pillowcases, and, of course, patchwork quilts. Quilting is an art form that permeates many cultures, each of which has its own special designs. It is still popular, probably because each quilt is unique and offers the opportunity to sew in a wealth of personal history. Many are created intentionally as heirlooms of the future, incorporating scraps of material from family clothes (especially children's) and household furnishings, which will become a permanent reminder of times past.

Long may all these fabrics live in country homes, along with the talent to mix them indiscriminately – the old and the new, the fine and the functional, and the patterns and colors from East and West. This casual hodgepodge of different furnishings and decorative fabrics contributes so much to a country interior's informal charm.

LEFT *Roughly woven, undyed linens and dish towels typify the fashion for utilitarian fabrics in the contemporary country home.*

RIGHT *Off-white linen drapes and a white pillow allow the colors of the wooden dining chair, pine dresser, and painted window seat to take precedence in a dining room.*

Nature's color inspiration is at its

brilliant best here, with buckets of tulips

painted in an exciting riot of shades.

THE
ENTRANCE

Inside out and outside in

Life in the English countryside is lived between the two

RUNNING FROM FRONT DOOR to back and into all the corners of the country home is a network of pathways. These halls and stairways are the arteries of the house, linking the rooms and the life and activities played out within them.

The garden gate and the front door welcome visitors, the foyer invites them in, and the hallways provide a full introduction to the home. The impression they make is paramount; you only have to think about experiences of house- or apartment-hunting to realize that a decision about whether or not you would even consider living somewhere is made the second you walk through the front door. The all-important "feeling" of a house is instantly apparent, and some homes have a good feeling while others simply do not.

One of the secrets of achieving this is to let the feeling of daylight, fresh air, and indigenous materials of the natural world continue uninterrupted through the house. Pale paint colors or papers with simple patterns will help create a light and airy atmosphere, as will mirrors to reflect daylight, and lamps for after dark. Floors of stone, brick, tiles, or bare boards will also help soften the transition from the outside of the house deep into its interior. All these create an atmosphere that is relaxed and undemanding, bright and open, rather than dark and forbidding. The inside of the house will be a space in which you can breathe as easily as you can outside.

Another important part of this design equation, which is probably the most difficult, is the need to keep these areas relatively clutter-free. Too many odds and ends will not only look oppressive but will also prevent easy movement between the rooms. Therefore, throw away, or put away, everything you can, incorporate ingenious storage solutions into your home, and retain only those items that have to be there, so that their decorative qualities stem from their specific functions.

Here there is room to move: from a spacious glazed porch, through the door into the large entry hall leading to the adjoining downstairs rooms. Waxed terra-cotta tiles in warm, earth tones gleam in the light and connect the entry hall to the real earthiness just outside. This entrance manages to look both settled in and mellow, and modern and open, at one and the same time.

Exterior doors in country homes, front and back, often open straight into the action of the household. The first impression on entering may be a living room rather than an introductory foyer, and there may be no opportunity at the back door for a messy utility area. The decorating scheme of the house continues right to the boundary with the outside.

The practical solution can become the decorative touch with storage in foyers. A writing desk provides a useful place for the incoming mail; a table with drawers is also a display case,

with its bulletin board above; a bamboo hall stand shows off the accoutrements of rural sports; and a flower picture becomes a key holder. Much is still visible, but it is stored.

Flights of stairs are a decorating opportunity not to be missed – often the place for something a little fanciful. Stenciled or freehand murals, particularly painted to dado height, can make a stairway entertaining. Unusual shapes and materials, such as the brick combined with wood here, add considerable interest to an otherwise functional area.

There is not a carpet in sight, but the hard-surface floors that befit a country interior are varied and satisfyingly decorative. Differing, attractive effects are achieved in these interiors with old terra-cotta tiles and inset mosaic; painted wood in imitation of an oriental rug; well-mellowed quarry tiles; and pale new wooden floorboards.

THE GARDEN GATE AND FRONT DOOR

Somewhere in everyone's subconscious is an indelible image of the ideal country home. The garden gate, made of weathered wood or old wrought iron, swings gently in the breeze on its hinges. The garden blooms with herbaceous color in higgledy-piggledy manner, or bright zinnias and geraniums planted in old olive-oil cans brave the fierce glare of the midday sun. Gnarled trees droop with slowly ripening fruit. Wild forest or moorland surrounds the house, or the sea crashes at the foot of the cliffs beyond the safety of the garden wall. Wherever, exactly, we are in our imagined country world, the eye focuses on the front door of the house, always open and inviting.

The romance of these mind-pictures lies in the link they assume between nature outside and a natural lifestyle inside, and an ease of movement between the two. There exists in all cultures a strong desire to live in some working relationship with the natural world. This is the impulse behind the country-garden flowers of the living room chintz, and the terra-cotta tiles covering the kitchen floor. The open front door blurs the distinction between inside and out.

Today's architects, with modern materials and manufacturing techniques at their disposal, have taken this romantic idea several steps further. Entire

An unadorned laurel wreath and small colored lights are hung along an unpainted picket fence and through a red-berried cotoneaster, adding an effortless magic and mystery to this entrance. With its simplicity and lack of frills, the arrangement conjures up the pagan traditions which predate Christmas and celebrate the winter season.

exterior walls of glass erode the boundary between inside and out, so that the inhabitants of some spectacular modern country houses are effectively living in the landscape. Other architects have ingeniously designed homes sunk beneath the ground, their subterranean structures hardly interrupting the natural contours of the land above, the windows looking straight up at the moving clouds. These modern homes are a far cry from traditional plump chintz-covered sofas, but they are in a similar vein, developed with the same hope of a symbiotic relationship between the inside and outside rural worlds, the idea of the open front door taken to its most extreme resolution.

In the bricks and mortar of everyday life, the setting of the country home may not be quite as perfect as it is in the mind's eye, but the essence of the dream can

LEFT *The rather austere lines of this brick farmhouse are offset by the Mediterranean blue of the window frames. The color is pulled through the garden to the blue gate by the thick growth of lavender and rosemary.*

RIGHT *The modest way in to a flintstone cottage is littered with standard trees and shrubs in terra-cotta pots and is home to free-range bantam hens. A bent willow bough creates an arch from which to hang tin lanterns.*

still be realized. Perhaps the most important consideration of all is that the house should seem at ease. The fabric of the building and its colors should be in sympathy with the surroundings. If it is to relate to the natural world, the country home cannot put up a visual fight.

This is not a problem if you are lucky enough to live in a house built from local stone or brick that seems to blend into the landscape, or perhaps in a modern glass-walled house on stilts hidden high in a pine forest. But if you don't, you may need to disguise rather than emphasize the exterior of your home. Using local colors is a good rule of thumb. A stroll around the area or a little historical research can reveal the traditional paint colors used on neighboring houses to cover brick or plaster and exterior woodwork. With a few cans of paint, a new house made from imported materials can be given a quick character change, so that it no longer looks a rank outsider.

The exterior of the country home is often defined by plants of one species or another. If there is an ancient wisteria overhanging the upstairs windows or a venerable grapevine scrambling over an adjoining pergola, you are fortunate. If not, then avail yourself of some fast-growing shrubs and climbers. Where these cannot be grown, a jumble of pots and containers can still be planted up. Anything goes, so long as it's green – from the colorful hollyhocks and nasturtiums of Victorian tea-plate repute, to the luscious architectural foliage more often found in urban roof gardens.

With the essentials in place and the outside of the house pleasing to the eye, the other senses can be indulged. Scented plants, such as a wonderful lavender hedge that you brush against as you walk up the path, are a lovely prelude to the home. The sounds of flowing water, of wind-chimes, of birds and bees attracted by flowers and berries, build on the link between the house and its surroundings. Twists and turns in a path, magical lighting after dark, and the rustling of foliage recreate some of the mystery inherent in nature.

The sum of all these parts ideally creates an atmosphere that is informal and unintimidating, one that puts approaching visitors at their ease rather than trying to impress. A touch of humor does not go amiss either, perhaps in the form of an entertaining statue or sculpture peeping from the undergrowth. Respect and understanding of the natural environment does not dictate solemnity.

Looking through the open front door of that imaginary country home, in your mind it is one of those unexpected warm and sunny days in the fall; muddy boots are flung in the porch and a basket of freshly harvested blackberries sits on the table, ready for jam-making. In the real world, by contrast, it is cold and raining and the door is firmly shut against the elements. Nevertheless, it will swing open with the greatest of ease to reveal a welcoming entry hall. And, just inside, there will indeed be flowers, home-grown produce, twigs, foliage – whatever – brought in from the garden in time-honored fashion.

Elements of surprise and humor are evident on this front door in a spectacular, twelve-pointed star knob and a ball-and-hand knocker emerging from a dainty sleeve. A Delft-tiled stove makes a novel table, and the contrasting paintwork colors exploit the ecclesiastical-style architecture of the house.

LEFT *Life is clearly being enjoyed in this country home. A bicycle laden with market produce has arrived in the foyer, and the stone entrance and sturdy old polished floorboards are robust enough to accommodate the traffic.*

RIGHT *Sunlight floods through the front door, and the brick paving of the path outside continues straight into the house, linking the interior and exterior architecture and the life in the house with that in the garden.*

THE ENTRY HALL

The entry hall provides the first impression of the feel and style of the home – a preview of what might lie beyond. When the entry hall is decorated in a warm, airy, and lively way, the rooms leading off it are assumed to follow suit and be equally inviting. But if the foyer is cold and austere, or merely a thoroughfare of junk and dark corners, it will not seem an attractive context for the living style of the home.

Too often, the entry hall is neglected for years, its true character considered only after all the other rooms are decorated. It is also a prime dumping ground for all sorts of clutter not wanted elsewhere, absent-mindedly deposited by family members as they enter the house. Yet the

secret of creating a successful introduction to the home is to treat the entry hall just as seriously as any other room, thinking of it as a space that is lived in, not one that is just hurried through.

The real, working home in the country, in almost any location and at any point in history, has never been seen with a wall-to-wall carpet or expensive oriental rugs on its entry hall floors. The first consideration for a country foyer has always been practicality. Living and working in the country entails dirt, be it wet, sticky mud or dry, sun-baked dust, so floors that can be swept and washed clean easily are the best option. This style of practical, hard flooring endures in country homes today, whether the worker on the land has come inside from a modest vegetable patch or from a field full of cabbages.

LEFT *This cottage entry hall is designed with minimal decoration, but a good-size window lights up the flagstones and an old stoneware flagon, showing off their simple beauty.*

RIGHT *A magnificent, solid mahogany case-clock in this entry hall takes on a surprising lightness when juxtaposed with colorwashes of fresh spring greens and blues, which are taken across the ceiling and intensified in the shade used for the woodwork of the door.*

Hard flooring materials used in country entry halls are normally stone, brick, quarry tile, or wood, although terra-cotta and marble tiles have also been used for this purpose for centuries in southern Europe. All these are natural materials, looking their best when quarried or manufactured locally, so that their appearance inside the home seems entirely appropriate, in keeping with the surrounding landscape and the geographical area as a whole. For example, local stone used for a garden path (and for the garden walls) may continue uninterrupted right through the front door and into the hall; the same stone may also be seen occurring naturally in the garden and in the countryside beyond. Here, again, is the link between inside and out, this time at its most practical: in the days before vacuum cleaners, the dirt could simply be swept straight out through the front door.

The subdued colors of brick, stone, quarry tiles, and wood mellow with age and become more beautiful still. No other floorings can compare with stone worn down and polished in places by the tread of working boots, or with old oak boards gleaming with countless coats of beeswax. Nevertheless, new hard flooring materials are sophisticated and often stunning, and a modern country home can look marvelous with, for instance, bleached beechwood floors. Even some good-quality vinyls, sometimes cunningly disguised as something more natural such as slate tiles or marble, can look authentic; and they also have the added bonus of being immensely practical.

Often the most persistent and frustrating problem encountered in foyers and passageways is that of insufficient natural daylight, particularly in older country homes; when these houses were originally built, lighting and comfort in the conduits leading from one part of the house to another were not top priorities; cold, dark passageways were designed to be scurried along, carrying a scuttle of coal between one hearthside and the next. A light, open, modern style – made possible, above all, by the luxury of contemporary heating systems – demands far more daylight than is usually forthcoming.

The simplest solution to maximize the natural light in foyers and hallways is to glaze, or part-glaze, exterior and interior doors. Glass doors deserve a better reputation since an enormous range of attractive reinforced glass is now available, and there are many crafters producing stained glass.

Another device is the strategic positioning of mirrors that draw in more light from the outside, and bounce it back and forth within the confines of the hall. A foyer or hallway naturally presents itself as a gallery

LEFT *The restricted use of a floral wall-paper, only below the chair rail, makes this entrance pretty without overstating the idea.*

BELOW *The yellow walls of the foyer and stairway pick up the warm tones of the parquet floor of the adjacent dining room, visually linking the two areas.*

These foyers show how touches of color can be added to the subdued tones of natural decorating

materials by a few pieces of furniture or a limited number of accessories.

BELOW *A hall chair, a grandfather clock, and an armoire with a hint of bright color.*

BELOW RIGHT *A long, narrow table with fruit, flowers, and a picnic-hamper at the ready.*

space, and the work on display could be a collection of mirrors that are functional as well as decorative.

Creating a new window is a possible option, although it should not detract from the integrity of the exterior architecture. Skylights, often invisible from the outside, are perhaps a more attractive proposition and they can make a spectacular difference to a house. Suddenly there is sunlight pouring down from above, or perhaps a view of the clouds as you climb the stairs.

Artificial lighting in entry halls allows you to create the level of illumination that best complements the house, its atmosphere, and its decorative style. It can be used to soften any transitions in light quality between the adjoining rooms, and also to ensure that any awkward corners or unexpected steps or changes in floor level are well lit. Wall-fixtures and spotlights can be used to create mysterious shadows, illuminate pictures, or bathe a sitting or working area with plenty of light for the tasks in hand. Up-lighters could reflect off a low, pale ceiling to give the illusion of space and height; and a chandelier or elaborate lantern could look its magnificent best here.

For the majority of people, the most important part of entry hall decoration (which is, of course, connected with the amount of natural light) is the use of paint colors, and how to get the color equation right. The color in an entry hall, particularly on the walls and ceiling, has, somehow, to achieve so many ends: it must make the area look light and open, lend warmth, and provide a good transitional color between the rooms the entry hall gives on to. Then there are the large areas of woodwork – miles of baseboards and a far greater number of doors than there are in other rooms.

As a starting point, look at the colors you have, or intend, for the downstairs rooms adjoining the entry hall. This will narrow your choice immediately, because you should not choose a hall color that clashes badly with these – you will want something that either tones or contrasts pleasingly. If you can find colors that link the rooms and entry hall along a color spectrum, or within a tonal range, the result can look wonderful, lending the colors throughout the house a sense of continuity. Or you might go for a bright, definitive color to bring the whole area alive.

Success with color can, of course, never be guaranteed, but the most foolproof options here are pale colors that reflect light, rather than absorbing it. Bearing in mind the link between the house and the natural world outside, and the earthy tones of hard floorings, those light colors should perhaps be in naturally occurring shades – the greens and blues of foliage and water and sky, for example, or the grays, pinks, and beiges of stone and pebbles. Less natural, acid colors are difficult to get right. As a rule, the ceiling should be even lighter; a dark color will optically lower it, and no hall ceiling can be too high.

Additional entry hall color can then come from the things that have to be there or from the odd decorative accessory (but not too many) that you choose to add. Highlights of the natural tones will come from wooden picture frames, chairs, walking sticks, leather boots, wicker

A color scheme of red, light blue, and dull yellow pulls the eye through this hallway into the living room beyond, effectively disguising the fact that the hall is in fact quite dark and narrow.

baskets. Accents of sympathetic color can be added by the occasional faded old kilim or rag-rug, and by curtains or pillows made from natural fibers. The whole effect can be simple, but not spartan, carefully thought out but seemingly casual, a mixture of ideas and objects that relate to lives being lived rather than appearing out of the blue like props on a formal stage-set.

One reason there is such a tendency for odds and ends to accumulate in foyers and hallways is that in these areas of a home it is convenient to have all sorts of things accessible. Coats and hats and umbrellas are useful near the front or back door; house keys, car keys, the neighbors' keys need to be on hand; while outgoing or incoming mail and notes to other members of the household are best left at a juncture where they will be noticed. Bicycles, roller-skates, homework books, sports bags, the pot plant to take to a friend…the trouble is that the foyer can quickly begin to resemble a garage sale.

The entry hall is often in dire need of storage. It may be wide enough to accommodate a table with drawers or a long chest in which many of these things can be stored, or there may be space under a stairway which can be designed with shelves and coat hooks. A smaller entry hall might benefit from narrow wall shelves, hooks for keys or a discreet stand for coats, walking sticks, and the like. It will give greater peace of mind if the entrance to the house is an area of comparative calm rather than a reminder of the potential chaos of domestic life. Most of us would rather encounter a bowl of fresh flowers from the garden than three months' worth of household bills strewn on a table.

Walls at one end of this living room have been taken out so that thre is access to the room from either side of the fireplace. The wood paneling is painted in the same blue as the doors of the entry hall. Opening up the space and keeping the color scheme consistent in this way achieves a feeling of ease of movement between one living area and another.

LEFT *A short run of steps is enhanced by a painted mock baseboard and plain white walls. The pale green walls and the polished oak boards of the hallway beyond are enticing.*

RIGHT *Pastel shades, unsophisticated bare wood, and a rag rug are used as upstairs decoration in a modest cottage.*

THE STAIRWAY

Stairways come in all shapes and sizes – steep and narrow, shallow and wide, sweeping or boxed in, highly visible or completely hidden behind a latched door. They may consist of little more than a few steps leading up to the mezzanine level of an apartment, or they may aspire to being the central feature of a house, marching up to a grand, overhanging landing. Not only are stairways extremely varied in character, but their decorative treatments can be equally multifarious.

There are, however, three safety requirements all stairways have in common – that they are well lit, they are free of impediments, and there is some sort of handrail in place. If natural light in this part of the home is poor, good artificial lighting needs to be installed and used during the day and at night. Ideally, the lighting should be designed so that the depth and rise of each step are clearly visible. Tempting though it may be, it is generally best to resist putting any object at all on a staircase, unless it is up high on the wall. The handrail may take the form of a banister or merely a rope securely attached by rings to the wall, as long as it is something to catch hold of. Even the completely able-bodied stair climber can feel insecure if there is no rail at all.

A stairway is rarely a completely separate entity, but is part of the flow of the foyer and hallways that run through the house. Usually the wall of the stairs is a continuation of the entry hall below and of the landing at the top, so it is likely to be decorated in the same way, or at least so that it provides a gentle transition between the styles of decoration in these two areas. The exception to this is a staircase with such character that it begs for a little decorative panache to make it a major feature of the house.

The treads on the stairway are the largest decorating consideration. Within the scheme of the

open, airy country home, they are left as clear of carpet as the other parts of the foyer and hallway network. Their wooden boards may be fine enough to polish and leave bare, or they could be painted over. Even just a coat or two of roughly applied white paint can look charming and can be a cheap, simple and quick solution if the boards are less than perfect (coat them with flat varnish to prevent scuff marks).

If the stairs are in bad condition or are unsafe, they may need to be replaced, in which case there are a lot of attractive options, from pale new woods to open metalwork. In certain situations, sheer practicality will dictate the style. There is nothing quite like the sound of several small children thundering up and down an old, bare, wooden staircase to give you a sudden renewed taste for carpets (as the wind whistling up through the gaps from a basement below might, too). A carpet or rug runner that goes up the middle of the stairs, leaving a wide polished or painted edge either side, can solve the problem. And there are all the sisals and seagrass mattings, although these need to be of good quality and carefully fitted, as they can stretch out of shape and become dangerous on the stairs.

The dark woods and the apple green and cream paints of this little stairway give it a distinctly 1950s' appearance. A length of ship's rope provides a simple handrail.

The green and cream decoration continues through the hall and into a fresh-looking room. An old central-heating radiator is painted white to emphasize its sculptural qualities.

Stairways often provide a great opportunity for paint effects, ranging from subtle faux finishes to wildly over-the-top trompe l'oeil murals. A large expanse of wall can look blank, and may benefit from being divided up by a real or trompe l'oeil chair rail, with different color, texture, or pattern on either side. Similarly, a deep baseboard can be painted to contrast with the walls, or a false one painted onto the wall. Above all, such devices emphasize the shape of an attractive stairway, particularly the sweep of a curving inner wall. Alternatively, the minimalist may relish the idea of a huge, simple shape of wall painted white and otherwise completely untouched by decorating hand. The treads of the stairway, if not carpeted, offer scope for paint effects – the risers, for example, could be stenciled with folk-art motifs.

Front gate, front door, foyer, stairs, landing, and hallways – all lead, in the end, to the back door. In our imaginations, this, like the front door, will remain open, a light summer breeze swaying the kitchen curtains, the sound of birdsong drifting into the house, the perfume of herbs and flowers giving an edge to the air. The country home is restful, easy on the eye, and connected throughout to the landscape beyond.

At the back door, the country kitchen and its garden are in perfect partnership. The cabinets are painted a bluish-green while the rough plaster of the walls is colorwashed in bright, sunny yellow. A decorative Indian textile pinned above the door filters the bright light pouring in from outside. The flowering plants on the inside windowsill help to pull the garden into the house, breaking the boundary between inside and out.

LIVING
SPACES

The core of the home

Where the living is easy and informal

THE KITCHEN, DINING ROOM, AND LIVING ROOM are the communal spaces of a country home, where family and friends gather. The rooms must accommodate all the disparate practicalities of day-to-day life and yet be places in which guests feel welcome and relaxed. As these rooms have to take on so many different roles, their decoration and furnishings require close attention. Comfort, practicality, and informality are the three things we can aim to achieve here, and strong lines, clear colours, and a carefully calculated casualness are key ideas when approaching their interior schemes.

Because most of the household activities take place in these rooms, they are not places where people will stand on ceremony. Instead, they should be designed for ease of living – rooms that are open and as full of light and fresh air as possible, and between which you can move freely. Ideally, the furnishings will have evolved gradually over a period of time, settling down into an unobtrusive style that looks natural and uncontrived. Foreign artifacts sit comfortably alongside more traditional country furniture, and old pieces complement the new.

Natural materials and organic color tones are as important here as elsewhere in the country home, because of the strong connection between the rooms and the landscape outside. The most important framed scenes – in kitchen, dining room, and living room alike – are the views through the windows.

LEFT *The idea of living in one room is revolutionized here by the brilliant use of a small space: the kitchen, dining, and living rooms and platform bedroom even manage to look spacious.*

RIGHT *These custom-built cabinets show the value of reclaimed wood – the inimitable glow and patina of age. Exposed bricks make a perfect backdrop.*

Nothing can quite match the pulling power of an open fire, of logs crackling in the grate or lighting up the glass door of an old stove. A fire inevitably becomes the focal point of any

room, and a much more attractive and relaxing one than the television set that seems to have taken over this role in many a town house.

Paint effects are about transformations: of an old door, of a decorative armoire, of a plain fireplace, and of a storage chest that becomes a 1950s' period piece for its pair of wire-haired

fox terriers. Paint them freehand if you have the skill, or use stencils and masking tape if you need more guidance.

The great thing about contemporary storage solutions is that they look good, as designers have tackled the subject with a vengeance. Old shop fittings provide inviting little drawers,

lidded baskets are now widely available, and freestanding kitchen furniture has undergone a fashion revival.

A collection may be of fine china, rustic earthenware, practical tinware, or anything you please. The approach to its display is informal, on open shelves in a kitchen rather than behind glass cabinet doors in the parlor. The pieces in the collection are for use, or at least suggest that they might be.

THE KITCHEN

The kitchen of the country home has come to represent much more than merely the space where food for the household is prepared and stored. It stands as a symbol of the very essence of the home – the place where friends and family meet and talk, eat, and relax, where they come to get warm, both literally and metaphorically. It is a room with many different functions, all of which flourish in an atmosphere of easy informality.

Security, comfort, and stability are at the root of this romantic image of the country kitchen, which provides a focal point in hectic lives. In the cottage kitchen,

LEFT *White, apple green, and pale turquoise make up a gentle color backdrop in this modest kitchen. The floor is paved with York stone and the dining table and schoolroom chairs are made from a variety of hard and soft woods. Touches of harmonizing color are provided by earthenware pitchers and vases in one-color glazes.*

BELOW *Another view of the kitchen shows an Aga range in the same pale turquoise shade and a collection of contrasting bright blue ironware cooking pots. The brickwork in the Aga alcove has been left unplastered and is painted white, and the only other decoration is in the pot of metal utensils and the wall-mounted wire container.*

particularly, a wood-burning stove (or its more recent equivalent, the radiant heat Aga range) is always lit; wooden chairs and a settle are strewn with colorful cushions; a sturdy dresser holds a collection of pretty china; and plates are displayed around the room at picture-moulding height. As a result of the strong identity it has developed over the years, this paradigm has become something of a style caricature and is now to be found in many parts of the Western world. Its key elements have been mass-produced and introducd into thousands of kitchens in houses of all architectural styles in cities, towns, countryside, and suburbs alike, whether they are truly appropriate or not.

Inevitably, the elements of the original style have been watered down and misunderstood. The beautiful pitch-pine dresser, proud possession of a modest rural household a century ago, is unsuccessfully reinvented in the plastic-pine veneer of crudely molded kitchen cabinets. Simple fabrics such as gingham are used for ruffles and frills in window treatments that bear little resemblance to the original uses of such materials. Once-attractive styles slowly mutate into oppressive fashions. A similar fate awaits Shaker style; as it is repackaged supposedly to suit modern tastes, the whole philosophy of the Shaker way of life, reflected in the simplicity and superb craftsmanship of the sect's homes, is fast being reduced to represent nothing more than a palette of paint colors.

Kitchen design is not the only area of interior decoration to be subject to these corruptions, but it is perhaps the one where the results are the most obvious. There is now a growing reluctance to go on repeating such design clichés, and a willingness to peel away excess decoration and return to a more honest appraisal of simple country kitchen elements. Because few people are prepared to give up the benefits of their microwave ovens, food processors, dishwashers, and other modern conveniences, designers are now coming up with inventive ways of combining old features with high technology. The attempt to make the country kitchen not only warm and cozy but also clean-lined and state-of-the-art is leading to some excellent design ideas.

The essential homeliness and basic components of the ideal country kitchen are still in place today, but they have been stripped of some of the pretentions that have grown up around them over the years. With the exposure of brick and rough plaster and the cutting back of ornamentation, the new country kitchen style is paying tribute to an even earlier model. While the typical "cottage" look is essentially Victorian, not much more than a hundred years old, rough plaster goes back several centuries earlier. Paradoxically, in imitating a truly antique

RIGHT ABOVE *A wall-mounted cupboard and kitchen dresser have been treated with a variety of paint effects using shades of turquoise and sandstone. The kitchen utensils and earthenware on display, all dating from the 1950s, also show a predominance of greens and yellows.*

RIGHT BELOW *Reclaimed wood, with much of its original paint still clinging on, has been used here to great effect in the creation of wooden cabinetry. Touches of bright scarlet red in the paint are emphasized by the brand new range and by the surfaces of polished wood. The walls are roughly colorwashed in ocher. A tall, thin central-heating radiator is given the status of fine sculpture.*

look, this stripped-back style appears more "modern." This is largely because the textures of the materials used to build the kitchen, and the revealed shapes of the room, are more evident than they were when they were hidden behind layers of decoration and superfluous ornamentation. Simple forms, which may originally have been created out of bare necessity, seem modern to us.

The paint colors that are used to decorate the contemporary country kitchen tend to be characteristically cool and restful, as the kitchens illustrated on these pages demonstrate. Blues and greens predominate, from distinctive royal blues to indistinct turquoises, often combined with muted sandstone yellows. Soft whites, creams, and grays provide the backdrop to these stronger shades. The country kitchen is no longer characterized by a riot of color – it has more to do with the cool spectrum of the seashore than with the cheerful confusion of the fairground.

It is surprising how good these colors can look used in seemingly random combinations. A grass green can sit alongside an ocean turquoise, or an intense sky blue next to a sandy yellow. As long as they are all drawn from the same tonal range, the color partnerships can be quite daring and will still work well. These colors can be applied in solid areas to give clean, fresh lines, or they may be laid one on top of the other and rubbed back to give the time-worn look that is now so familiar. Better still, perhaps, leave battered painted furniture and cabinets just as they are, so they do not look too pampered in what is fundamentally a utilitarian room.

Similarly, the walls of the kitchen can be left in their original faded state or washed over with limewash or colorwash, producing an appearance that is not too finished, and that celebrates any imperfections in the surfaces rather than trying to disguise them. Precision is not always called for in an environment that is about ease of living and doing.

A striking pair of windows has been left as the main design statement here. All that was then needed was the fine carpentry of the simple rows of shelves and of the specially designed kitchen cabinetry.

This utilitarian approach can also be exploited in the equipping of the kitchen. Simple utensils – either of elderly faded tin or of brand-new stainless steel – usually come in beautiful shapes and are decorative in their own right. Ironwork fixtures or angular metal shelves look simultaneously graphic and pretty against cool-colored walls and woodwork. Painted tinware jugs and storage containers look entirely appropriate in this decorative context.

LEFT *A Shaker-inspired cupboard and peg rail work well in this kitchen where decoration and display are kept to a minimum. In keeping with the style, useful kitchen objects are hung up out of the way, and the cupboard contains simple creamware and dish towels.*

RIGHT *An enamel-topped table accommodates a painted tin bread box, its color picked up in the paintwork of the cupboard above. The wooden ceiling beams and stone window lintel contrast with the plain white-painted walls, and little else is needed to decorate this kitchen corner.*

In a pared-down country kitchen, contemporary designs, even of the most functional objects, often look more sympathetic and even exciting. Central-heating radiators, extractor fans, stainless-steel sinks, modern faucets and sleek new ranges fit into the scheme of things surprisingly successfully. The fridge and the dishwasher do not need to be hidden behind wooden panels to make them look like part of the kitchen cabinetry, but can stand proud as objects that are worth looking at. When the key elements of the interior involve materials, form, and function rather than pattern and ornamentation, it is much easier to combine items from widely different eras. In fact, real energy can result from the juxtaposition of old pieces and new technology.

There is a risk that in abandoning the strictures of the old cottage kitchen style, they will be replaced by new ones that carry even more of a design fervor – and a purist, austere one at that. A humorless environment is not a relaxed one. It is far better for the creators of the kitchen to allow personal and sentimental touches to remain. In the country kitchen there will always be a place for that pitcher of flowers on the table.

Two examples of kitchen ceramics show differing tastes and styles.

FAR LEFT *A comprehensive collection of blue-and-white striped 1950s' Cornishware looks entirely appropriate on a distressed turquoise dresser of the same period.*

ABOVE LEFT *Traditional cottage style is typified by this pine dresser stocked with everything from ceramic sheep and dogs to spongeware.*

THE DINING ROOM

The desire to escape from the town or city and to run for the country, whether in fact or only in spirit, carries with it the wish to leave rigidly polite living practices behind. The idea of a formal dining room with table perfectly set for a sophisticated dinner party (which has taken days to plan and to prepare) is anathema to the devotee of country living.

In many country homes, the dining room and the kitchen are, in any case, one and the same space, an arrangement that makes formal eating plans impossible. A solid farmhouse table next to the stove is for practical meals served without the trimmings. Where dining can take place in an entirely separate room, it is characteristically still decorated in an easy, relaxed manner; the tablecloth (if there is one at all) is more likely to be gingham than starched linen. The ideal atmosphere in a country dining room is one where friends can relax and talk, with few demands made

ABOVE *A huge fireplace in the corner is flanked by a pair of low, armless, upholstered chairs, perfect for taking an aperitif. The deep yellow-ocher walls give a sunny look to this pretty room.*

RIGHT *A daringly bright pink used on the walls of this dining area is offset by the color tones of the dark gray-green used for the woodwork. Both colors are picked up in a simple gingham tablecloth.*

In a house in the South of France, a tall window is open to the elements and to a view of the mountains of Provence. The sunshine is cheerfully echoed by the orange-painted walls. Cut wildflowers are ready for arranging in an earthenware pitcher.

upon them – one where the diners are not required to impress and the decor of the room does not attempt to do so, either.

Country dining room style is, in fact, a good example of how decoration signals the ways of living and behaving that take place within the walls of a room. Decorations and furnishings can actually dictate the lifestyle. Implicit in a floor of stone, tiles, or bare boards, for example, is the fact that any dropped crumbs can be quickly swept away, and that a spilt glass of wine is not a disaster. As a result, guests feel much more relaxed that they would if their feet were resting on an expensive, cream-colored carpet or a Persian rug.

If the dining room is not actually part of the kitchen, there is still probably easy access between the two spaces, through an open door or an archway, perhaps; the preparation and cooking of the food are left visible, not treated as a domestic secret to be kept hidden. A dish towel, which would never be seen in a town dining room, will find its way into its country cousin equivalent and not look out of place.

Plain wooden dining furniture, without upholstery, is indicative of a country mood. Whereas soft, upholstered chairs in matching sets are for more formal dining rooms, in the rustic home it is not only permissible but even preferable to have a number of unmatched dining chairs, each with its own character, or each to meet the sitting preferences of a different member of the family. Wooden seats polished with use to a comfortable shape, time-worn wickerwork, straight-backed chairs with rush seats – all these are typical. The dining table, which is often round, may be quite small, immediately obviating the possibility of inviting large numbers of people to dinner. Its size and distressed surface make it more suited to having a few close friends to supper.

Little else is really necessary in the dining room – perhaps nothing more than a painted cupboard containing glasses (simple tumblers rather than fine cut crystal), tableware, and flatware. If the cupboard is flush to the wall, built into an alcove in utilitarian fashion, so much the better. There may be a dresser, instead, or a few wall-mounted shelves, or one or two baskets used as storage containers.

Paint colors in a dining room where easy, intimate meals are eaten are best taken from a warm palette of creams, yellows, ochers, terra-cottas, pinks, and oranges. Any one of these makes the room appear welcoming and will also bring out the depths of tone in the wooden furniture. These rich tones look fantastic painted straight over uneven brick, stone, or plaster, making a virtue of the irregularities and casting light and shadow.

Cool colors from the blue and green spectrum as a backdrop to basic furnishings might make a dining room appear somewhat spartan and unfriendly, though in the kitchen this scheme can work well (see page 86). It is not really necessary to make the quality of light in the dining room particularly bright, unless tasks that require good illumination, such as reading, writing, and sewing, are also going to take place here.

The look of such country dining rooms is natural, earthy, and wholesome, like the food to be eaten in them. The guest here is confident of a hearty and healthy meal, probably incorporating fresh seasonal produce from the garden, and does not feel at risk of an over-styled and skimpy plate as he might in an elaborate town room. The decorations connect with the food, which once again highlights the idea of the outdoors brought into the home.

The feel of the room may change quite radically from day to nighttime and from season to season. It can accommodate a summer lunch taken by an open window, with the scent of herbs coming in from the garden; and, equally, it will adapt to the needs of a winter supper eaten by candlelight. Certainly, the lighting in the dining room should

French doors at the other end of the dining room open onto a patio, where another table is placed for eating out of doors. A large dresser and a full-height cupboard are stacked with unglazed pots and bowls and with baskets.

enhance the atmosphere created by the food, be it crisp, cold salads or warming bowls of soup.

A dining table is a wonderful opportunity for lighting directly from above, drawing the main focus in on the meal being shared. The light could be an antique lantern that can be lowered to the right height; a plain metallic, down-lighting, modern shade; or a gothic wrought-iron candelabra. Wall sconces holding more candles, or one or two electric wall lights, extend the dining mood out to the edges of the room and highlight the rich wall colorings.

The decoration of the rural dining room, then, sets a mood that is friendly, straightforward, and undemanding. It creates an eating environment which will tolerate children as happily as adults, and which leaves the constraints of city entertaining far behind.

A cool dining room is dominated by a magnificent carved stone fireplace and a glazed built-in cabinet. The romantic chandelier is based on a folk-art design. Cream-painted woodwork contrasts with the richly polished floorboards and dining table.

ABOVE *If there is such a thing as sophistication in country dining, it is evident here in contemporary oak furniture.*

RIGHT *A trompe l'oeil door, worthy of a child's illustrated storybook, leaves no doubt about the location of the pantry.*

THE LIVING ROOM

LEFT *A clever mix of fabrics provides the decorative personality here. The sofa is upholstered in white-on-white patterned linen, the armchairs in wide checks. Tie-dyed fabric covers the table and acts as a throw. Even the firescreen matches.*

BELOW *Pale on pale is used here, in the stone of the fire surround, the peppermint walls, and the woodwork. Wooden floorboards, logs, and wood boxes add a soft earthiness to the room.*

One of the incomparable charms of rural living rooms is that they are uncontrived, developing their style and content gradually and randomly over a period of time. What could, as a result, be a hodgepodge of odds and ends of furniture and decorative items in fact somehow acquires a coherence. The country living room at its best is that most enviable of interior achievements, a collection of different pieces that appear to be thrown together but nevertheless look great.

The inspiration for this form of effortless decorating can be found outside the doors of the home, in the country garden. Here, flowering plants are allowed to self-seed and pop up wherever they take root, yet the whole mix looks natural and organized. The secret of this style – whether in the garden or in the home – is precisely in its apparent lack of planning.

The decorative approach to the living room can be explained by extending the garden metaphor. First, there is the groundwork, the preparation of the

soil (or the room's backdrop) in which the flowers (or furnishings) will eventually grow. Most of the rooms pictured here, for example, have started out with a basic skeleton of hard floorings – stone, tiles, or bare boards – and little more than a coat of white or off-white paint applied to the walls and ceilings. The irregularities on these surfaces are not ironed out but just accepted into the scheme of things: the paint is simply applied over rough bricks or imperfect plaster. White or another pale color provides an unimposing background to the room's furnishings, and adds to its feeling of lightness and airiness.

The next consideration is the fundamental elements of the room which will provide a structure around which any furnishing confusion can safely occur – the wonderful, rural looseness of effect needs a firm framework in place. Again, this emulates cottage gardening practices, where a few "architectural" plants give shape to a relaxed planting scheme and visually contain the profusion of flowers that grow up through them.

ABOVE *Walls, ceiling, floorboards, and wooden settle are all treated with very light, harmonizing colorwashes in this country living room.*

LEFT *Strong shades of red and orange frame a fine old wood-burning stove.*

In the living room, the structure is provided by the existing, integral architectural features, such as the fireplace, windows, and doors.

A fireplace is a natural focus to a room. Perhaps it is of beautiful old stone that can be cleaned and restored. Alternatively, it may be an old farmhouse stove, or it could be a streamlined, modern fireplace designed for open wood burning.

The windows of the room are perhaps its most important, defining feature. The view through them to the garden and the filtering in of natural light can open up the living room to a relationship with the natural world outside, exploiting its rural context. If the design of the windows and their trim is attractive, it may be preferable to keep any drapes or other treatments clear of the whole area of the windows, so that the windows themselves can be fully appreciated. Possibly the windows do not need shades or drapes at all, particularly if they are not overlooked from outside; or shutters or venetian blinds may look better. In any case, window treatments in a country living room are best kept simple – made from undyed linen, for example, or from a white-on-white or pale-colored crewelwork, or from other neutral fabrics. The curtains can hang from a wrought-iron pole or can consist of material simply flung or twisted over a wooden pole at the top. The rural living room is not the place for heavy brocades or for swags, tassels, and trimmings; it needs instead something simple that can billow in the wind.

Doors to the room could be stripped of old paintwork if they are worthy of exposure, or painted to bring out the beadings or moldings. Any beams or ceiling rafters that create interesting angles and lines could be emphasized as part of the structure of the room. Other features that are part of the framework include any built-in cupboards, such as on either side of a fireplace. It is also important to plan lighting at this stage, particularly if wiring for wall lights needs to run down inside the walls. Alternatively, rafters may present a marvelous opportunity for a chandelier or lantern, or for a striking modern light fixture.

Once the outline of the room is in place, with its strong shapes and clean surfaces, it is ready for "planting out" with the furniture and decorative pieces that provide its easygoing, naturally evolving character. Now the fun starts. The best advice is to take things slowly, making no attempt to complete the furnishings of the room in one fell swoop: an instantaneous, inflexible arrangement is not what is needed. There will inevitably be a mix of existing furniture, perhaps sofas and chairs and chairside or cocktail tables, freestanding shelves and table lamps, which will go into the room straightaway. It is worth taking the time to move these around periodically and to see how they look in different positions in the room, rather than making an instant decision about their placement. It may be that one or two of the items meant for the living room in fact look better in another room of the house; or pieces may be swapped – for example, the chair in the bedroom for the chair meant for the living room.

Over a period of time, a great variety of furnishings find their way into the living room. One way in which a loose, informal style that is still full of interest is achieved is through a subtle mixture of simple fabrics. Surprisingly, traditional Western fabrics – such as faded crewelwork draperies – tone well with oriental kilims, Indian throws, woolen blankets, and even tie-dyed cottons. The color shades of all of these are muted and understated and they can work wonderfully together. There is something particularly rewarding about successfully combining materials of very different origins and contrasting patterns. If the color tones are sympathetic, and if there is enough space and simplicity in the backdrop of the room, a fabric mixture looks natural and engaging.

RIGHT ABOVE *The lines of the arched windows and doorway and the radiating ceiling rafters are allowed to stand out clearly in this white-painted room. The striking kilim covering the sofa is restricted to earth tones.*

LEFT *Old kilims have been used here as upholstery material, in a room that relies for effect on an open, natural color palette. No fewer than three pairs of French doors connect the room with the outside.*

RIGHT BELOW *Another view of the same room shows its effortless combination of an African sculpture, Chinese dragons, and a contemporary table lamp.*

The furniture too may be a mix of styles and centuries – perhaps a faded, upholstered chesterfield next to a wicker armchair, or a wooden settle combined with a contemporary leather-and-steel chair. The artifacts on display in the living room could be anything from tribal bowls and stoneware pots to modern sculptures and tapestry wall-hangings; from folk-art animal models or carnival pieces to plants and church candles in holders. They are brought together to constitute a coherent style by virtue of their strong shapes and outlines, and because they are all chosen by the owners of the room, reflecting a particular taste, however wide-ranging.

There is no sense of clutter here, but there is a feeling that pieces can just appear from time to time because they are beautiful to look at, because they are humorous, or because they are of some sentimental significance. As long as no single piece shouts out too loudly above the rest, the room will look as natural, unplanned, and satisfying as the finest country garden.

RIGHT *The exception that proves the rule – a sumptuous, colorful, bohemian living room. Although hardly understated, the shades used are still found in nature and are reminiscent of a hot-colored flower border.*

BELOW LEFT AND RIGHT *Warm, naturally pigmented paint colors are used in a converted English mill and in an Italian farmhouse.*

Gentle garden colors of pale yellow, soft green, and scrubbed wood create a feeling of springtime in this kitchen, emphasized by the bright daylight pouring through a high window. No one could feel ill at ease in this cheerful room.

RETREATS

A hideaway, a secret place to escape to

Somewhere to pause from a busy life

EVERYONE NEEDS TO RETREAT from the world and from other people once in a while, and the best country home has a private place to creep away to, be it a room within the house or a separate building. The retreat may be somewhere to work, make things, or paint – possibly even a serious, fully equipped home office or studio. Or it may simply be somewhere to relax and be self-indulgent, such as a bedroom or a luxurious bathroom. Indeed, the whole country home may be the retreat, the place to collapse gratefully after a week's hard work.

A retreat needs to have privacy, charm, calm, and sensuality if it is to be truly restorative. It has to satisfy the soul and the senses and to recharge the mind. The retreat will contain favorite things: well-loved colors and patterns, a trusty old paintbrush, the latest novel by a favorite author, aromatherapy bath oils – whatever it takes. Perhaps the family cat will demonstrate how to find the best possible spot in which to relax!

ABOVE *A glorious bedroom decorated by a bell-shaped mosquito net and richly coloured oriental textiles.*

LEFT *A dressing-room retreat is roughly limewashed in peppermint green. A chair sits in the sunlight, ready for a moment of quiet thought.*

Ablutions do not have to be taken in clinical surroundings: some decorative ideas are particularly suited to bathrooms. Collections of shells cry out to be displayed in close proximity to water; hot-house plants flourish in a steamy atmosphere; and personal photos and prints acquire a certain distinction when hung in the bathroom.

The appeal of linen and heavy country lace perhaps has something to do with the paradox of these fabrics appearing both old and crisp at one and the same time. They encapsulate

two different childhood romances, one of prettiness and the other of practicality — the idea of a woman's touch both in decoration and at the ironing board.

An informal room requires a similarly relaxed approach to its flower arrangements. Country home flowers are not made to stand up straight, but are allowed to spread and flop as they would in the wild, and garden or wild flowers are favored above florists' varieties. Containers are similarly simple: a glass tumbler looks more in keeping than a grand vase.

Country bed linen is meant to be lounged on, and is not made up of the sort of materials that you would not want to wrinkle. Solid-colored cottons and ginghams, plaid blankets,

lace, patchwork, and chintz are all appropriate in bedrooms that still feel romantic and that are daytime retreats just as much as sleeping places.

ABOVE *Sunshine yellow walls greet the day in this tiny bedroom. A painted nightstand is the only furniture, apart from the bed itself.*

RIGHT *Full nostalgia for the flower border is allowed in this room of roses – which appear on the walls, on the bed quilt, and in the owner's closet.*

THE BEDROOM

The most obvious choice of retreat in many homes – in fact, often the *only* choice – is the bedroom. That is where that we go for that short nap after Sunday lunch, to make the most intimate phone calls, or to snatch half-an-hour reading a novel. If all the other rooms of the home are used as communal spaces, our own bedrooms, or perhaps the attic spare room, may be the only means of escape. This is certainly the case if there are young children in the home, who often have no respect for the boundaries of privacy.

At one time, bedrooms tended to be dark, cold, and musty places, entered only after nightfall or for a quick change of clothes. But in modern homes with comparatively little living space, the bedrooms are no longer closed off during daylight hours. This is in part due to the luxury of affordable, controllable heating which extends to all rooms of the home. In earlier times, only the most affluent would run to the extravagance of lighting fires in bedroom grates at all hours of the day.

With more leisure time at our disposal, we are relearning the art of relaxation, which has somehow gotten lost in our busy and all too purposeful lives. Winding down after a difficult day no longer comes naturally to us, nor can many of us easily find the relief of falling instantly into the deep sleep that follows hard, physical labor. In order to acquire these skills, we need help from our immediate surroundings.

In recent years, more and more emphasis has been put on the calming properties of our homes – through interior color schemes and decorations, for example, and arrangements of furniture. The oriental art of feng shui, which dictates designs for living that facilitate ease of mind and spirit, has become of great interest to many people. And even more people are interested in commonsense ideas of decoration and

the ways to create a peaceful atmosphere that will help make our lives enjoyable and less complicated.

The rural bedrooms from various countries illustrated on these pages are not grand and plush, but neither are they purely functional and uncomfortable. The striking characteristic they all have in common is their simplicity, cleared of the paraphernalia of living. The few odds and ends they do contain are either decorative or pertinent to the relaxed tasks in mind. A few favorite pictures hang on the wall, along with a special postcard, photograph, or other memento; a beautifully shaped bowl or basket may be the only other accessory. The piles of books on hand have nothing to do with work but are there to be read for pleasure. Vases of wild flowers bring the countryside into the retreat, scenting the air. These rooms are comfortable in a way that has less to do with coziness than with an attractive spareness of effect.

The single decorative focus in all these bedrooms is the bed itself – the centerpiece, of course, of the room's relaxation activities. Here, tradition and rural fantasy remain shamelessly intact, almost completely unmodernized. An antique iron or brass bedframe still creates a striking effect. The straight lines, or the restricted curving patterns, of the metalwork appear both traditional and contemporary. The design is so successful that it will never go out of fashion. And we are loath to abandon the wonderful traditional bedspreads and covers which, like ancient teddy bears, offer all the comforts of stalwart old retainers in a shifting world.

Homes in which a floral sprig or a chintzy rose is banished from all the other room schemes still allow a quilt of pink roses. Even brutal modernists have the sense not to throw away a patchwork bedspread that has been painstakingly sewn by their grandmother using scraps from the clothes of countless family members. Romance and sentimentality are, quite properly, still allowed free rein in the bedroom.

Fabrics from other cultures, particularly from the Indian subcontinent, have become familiar components of country bedroom style, perhaps because they combine rich colors and abstract, pretty patterns with inexpensive fibers, such as thin cottons. They are exotic and modest at one and the same time.

Old, well-laundered linen sheets are the most comfortable to slip between and also look wonderful partnered with the heavy lace trimming of linen pillowcases and the appliquéd cut-outs of a pure white counterpane. They are all the more beautiful in an otherwise simply decorated room.

This has to be the bedroom of our dreams, and as such it proves the point of simple country style. The shapes of the walls, rafters, and ecclesiastical window, and the light and the trees outside, are what make it so desirable. The decoration and furnishings are as simple as can be, to avoid distracting from the beauty of the room itself.

LEFT *A scheme of white-on-white concentrates the eye on the sculptural qualities of the modern cane chair and the small collection of contemporary pots and bowls.*

ABOVE LEFT *A touch of formality in the blue-and-white stripes and gray walls is evident in a room suitable for a grand old bear, survivor of childhood adventures.*

ABOVE RIGHT *Blankets, sheets, and pillows in faded blue and mauve, flowers and checks are a comforting sight.*

The decoration of the walls, ceilings, and floors of countrystyle bedrooms is almost incidental; it is there to provide a backdrop to the star turn of the bed at center stage. Bright, white limewash or sunny colors from a warm spectrum of yellows, oranges, or reds are slapped on easily over rough walls and across rafters. Floors are taken down to unpolished wooden boards, without that need to create wall-to-wall warmth that was an obsession of decorators in the days before central heating. A colorful, though slightly faded, kilim or a few rag-rugs are thrown down near the bed to comfort bare toes in the morning.

A little painted cupboard, an alcove for hanging clothes, a sturdy old chest of drawers – any one of these will provide good storage. A painted wicker chair or a long-treasured armchair may be set near the window for daydreaming. If the setting of the home is rural, the ultimate pared-down luxury is the complete absence of shades or curtains. The windows may look out onto the leaves of a tree, and at night you can lie in bed and gaze up at the stars. In this ideal world, it will be warm sunshine that wakes you gently in the morning, not the blare of an alarm clock.

THE BATHROOM

The plumbed-in, indoor bathroom is only a few generations old, having been introduced at the end of the nineteenth century when plumbing and the heating of hot water became practicable in grander homes. The owners of the earliest bathrooms were anxious to show off their modernity rather than their decoration. The marvelous newfangled technology of interior bath and water closet was a source of wonderment. It may seem hard to believe that the proud home-owner would once have invited guests to come and view the plumbing, but it would certainly have been a greater source of nineteenth-century pride and status than the new wallpaper in the dining room. For decades a bathroom was a sign of considerable affluence.

As a result of its functional beginnings, bathroom style is traditionally rather cold, celebrating hygiene and practicality in the gleaming ceramic tiles and harsh lighting. Today we can take such accoutrements for

Filled with early-morning sunlight, this intimate master bathroom is as fresh and white as the peony and apple-blossom displayed in his-and-her glasses.

granted and also enjoy comfort and style. The technology of multihead progammable showers, whirlpool baths or Jacuzzis, and sinks designed to fit even the most awkward of spaces can be combined with the pleasing aesthetics and nostalgia of old clawfoot tubs and the romance of soft, flickering candlelight.

A hundred years or so after its first appearance, the bathroom has become a room for lingering in, and the ablutions that take place there a source of pleasure rather than a mere necessity. The bathroom at its best is a retreat, a relaxing room where the rigors of the day can be soaked away in a bath of aromatherapy oils, where fluffy towels are always at hand and hot-house plants flourish. Or perhaps it is a retreat from the rest of the family, a private bathroom with favorite objects on the shelf, free from the children's plastic ducks and boats which perhaps live in another bathroom, down the hall.

The bathroom retreat must be warm and it must be private: there is nothing relaxing about lying in the bath and developing goose bumps, nor

BELOW LEFT *A vintage tin bath is placed where it always would have been, in front of the open fireplace, but now has the added benefit of plumbed-in faucets.*

BELOW RIGHT *The piles of well-laundered antique linen in this enticing bathroom corner make possible the luxury of using one or two more towels than are strictly necessary.*

does it help to have to duck and dive in order not to be glimpsed through the window. But the decoration does not need to be of the cozy, wall-to-wall carpet kind. The rural bathroom is more likely to be characterized by a romantic primitivism, particularly in the choice of fixtures.

An old enamel bath, preferably free-standing so that its comforting round shape and pretty claw-feet are on view, is almost *de rigueur*. It is part of the selective nostalgia of bathroom style – the taking of attractive elements of the past and updating them with the benefits of modern technology. The old bathtub may have a modern hand-held shower and a new enamel surface, but it will retain its original good looks.

Lighting is particularly crucial in the lived-in bathroom and, again, can be composed of the best of the past and of the present. Strategically placed overhead lights, such as low-voltage halogen down-lights, and mirror lights for shaving or applying make-up can be complemented by candlelight, to be used on its own for the perfectly relaxing evening bath. The windowless, sleek, ultra-modern bathroom is for city living – the rural bathroom will instead have natural light filtering through to illuminate daytime bathing. It may be that the tub can be cleverly

LEFT *The ultimate in rural bathroom romance – after a bath you can step out onto the adjoining patio to dry off in the sunshine.*

RIGHT *Nothing could be simpler than this old tub in an unadorned bathroom, but the beautiful old candlestick and the lace-trimmed bathmat make you want to bathe there.*

positioned at an angle so that the bather can see out through a window to greenery but nobody apart from the birds can see back in.

Floorboards can be left bare, but should be well supplied with easily washed rugs and mats to catch the drips and save the feet. Decorative details can be borrowed from nature in the form of shells, plants, and flowers. A few earthenware pots or simple, utilitarian ceramics, attractive bottles of potions and lotions, and piles of towels and magazines complete an environment of uncomplicated ease.

In addition to its comforts and perfumes, the country bathroom has other points in its favor. However relaxing it is, and well supplied with chairs and stools, books and newspapers, it is primarily a room where one can spend time alone. It need not, decoratively speaking, be taken too seriously, and is often the room where people are prepared to put on display their sense of humor, their idiosyncrasies, and their fantasies in decorating, without inhibition.

The bathroom may be the place where you display an odd little collection of, say, glassware, models, or relics of your childhood. Or the room may take on an overall theme, the nautical being an obvious and attractive option, with its portholes, ropes, strident colors, starfish motifs, and model crabs and seagulls.

Often a bathroom is painted in colors that you might not dare to use elsewhere, or is given patterned wallpaper or paint effects that do not

LEFT *Vases, figurines, and animal models are on display in this jolly bathroom. Part of the fun is in the use of contrasting textures, such as the functional floor tiles and the rich velvet curtain at the window. Period pieces, like the old tin pitcher, sit easily with children's plastic toys.*

RIGHT *An old file cabinet is used here for bathroom storage. The bathtub is positioned so the bather can lie back and look out across the fields.*

appear as a decorating idea elsewhere in the home. Once fixtures and tiles are taken into account, little wall area is actually available for decorating, so the logic runs that you can go for the exotic and change it with comparatively little cost or trouble if it all goes wrong. Such small areas of wall are often found with enchanting amateur *trompe l'oeil* paintings, decorative murals, antiqued paint effects, or stamped or stenciled motifs, which make the bathroom great fun to be in.

The rural bathroom retreat really will lift the spirits. It has everything – romance, warmth, light, comfort, perfumes, amusement. And if it does have to incorporate plastic ducks and boats after all, maybe they can become part of an experience of secret, therapeutic regression.

LEFT *Light, traditional, and airy, this bathroom still has its idiosyncratic odds and ends, an open fireplace for the winter, and an old radio for entertainment.*

RIGHT *While most bathroom decorators choose blues and greens, for obvious reasons, this bathroom is successful because it goes to the opposite extreme. Luscious red strawberries are stamped randomly over the white walls, and the theme is continued in the bright pink curtain and fruit-scented bath soaps.*

THE STUDIO AND HOME OFFICE

Imagine a wonderful wooden home office-cum-studio in the middle of a jumble of flowers and trees: part wooden tree house and part fairy-tale Hansel and Gretel cottage. It is a dreamy rural retreat, set apart from the main house, yet it is all wired up for today's computer technology and electronic communication. It has nooks and corners and steps where you can sit with a cup of coffee enjoying the garden, idly pinching off a few dead flower-heads from the overflowing pots. You just know that if only this were your own private studio, you would have no problem getting down to work and accomplishing great things, because simply being there would immediately put you in the right frame of mind.

An artist's studio space is snatched from a large landing next to the guest room. A fold-down desk is ready as a surface for painting, while rolled-up pictures are stored on the shelves of the large workbench on the left. Framed pictures are hung or propped up wherever there is room.

The emotions this fantasy studio touches on are precisely those that make many people long to flee the city in favor of the country. We are sure that, if only we could escape the undue pressures of our lives and acquire the tranquility of a rural retreat, then our creativity would blossom to its full potential. We would be able to work in the way we desire.

For growing numbers of people, this dream has become reality; having escaped city life and nine-to-five jobs for at least some of the week, they work from home in the country, either part-time or full-time. Their studies and studios may be found within the home, or in an addition, or set apart in just such a garden retreat as the one described opposite. Of course, the studio-in-the-garden is a more practical option in a warm climate where freezing winter days are rare, but even in cold places it can either be used when weather permits or be heated to make it habitable all year round.

The designated work space may be extensive or it may just consist of a small corner of another room. Wherever it is, and whatever its degree of luxury, this is still an essentially personal area, to be used on one's own for the concentrated thought found only in solitude. It is a true retreat, the place where the other side of one's life is indulged and given a chance to develop.

RIGHT ABOVE *The harmonious greens of the plant and flower subjects of this artist's work are echoed in the furnishings of an old painted wooden table and chair and green linen curtain.*

RIGHT BELOW *The artist at work in Italy in his top-lit, open-air studio, full of plants and cooled by a small mosaic-tiled ornamental pool. This lovely space provides room for two works in progress.*

The feature that artists require above all others in their studios is good natural light, so that colors and textures are true and can be clearly seen. Part of the attraction of an outdoor studio is this quality of light, and the fact that the artist can work inside and out, wandering between the two. Here, too, there is greater proximity to nature, whose changing colors and forms are a source of inspiration. Inside the studio, the best daylight floods in from skylights directly above the working area – an arrangement that is obviously easier to achieve in a lean-to addition or in a separate building than in the main home itself.

At the opposite extreme to the studio where large oil paintings are created or a potter's wheel and kiln accommodated, is the desk or table, pushed up against a sunny window, where delicate watercolors are painted. This studio may be no grander than a few jars of water, a box of

LEFT *A sense of a colonial past endures in this writer's bay window of a living room. A silk cloth, paisley shawl, and plaid blanket hark back to the early twentieth century, as do the inkpot, quill, and antique typewriter.*

RIGHT *Up-to-date, but still easy on the eye, this white and scrubbed-wood writing corner is equipped with laptop computer, phone-fax machine, and canine assistant.*

colors and small brushes, and perhaps a chest of drawers stuffed with paper and natural specimens – shells, stones, barks, mosses – to work from. The romance of this retreat is embodied in the work table itself, a single piece of furniture that symbolizes the task in hand. Instead of paints, the table may have an author's typewriter or computer screen, but the principle is the same. Again, the area will benefit from good natural light and an attractive view through the window.

The decoration of a working space, whether studio or home office, outdoors or in, can be kept neutral and calming, in a style that is not distracting. Watered-down latex paint in pastel shades will make the most of the available light. The furnishings are usually characterized by a charming, rickety practicality. In addition to the all-important work table, the chief requirements are a favorite chair and plenty of storage. Plan chests, file cabinets, shelves on the wall, baskets, and boxes can all contain the tools of a particular trade or craft.

Many people find that a too pristine decorating scheme, with everything clean and neat and shining, tends to inhibit the creative mind. They need to be able to surround themselves with the odds and ends

LEFT *A dreamy retreat in the woods, complete with wooden deck for reading and cogitating. That great novel could definitely be composed here.*

BELOW LEFT *A reclaimed garden shed becomes a hideaway for a serious gardener. Propagation and planning go on into the night by the light of an oil lamp.*

BELOW RIGHT *Another shed is made eminently habitable as a home office. The garden implements, hung from pegs on the wall, look like pieces of sculpture.*

that serve as inspiration or reminders – notes stuck to the desk, postcards pinned on the wall, overspilling paints, tendrils of plants creeping in from the outside. The atmosphere of the work retreat can be one of organized chaos, where the book or the drawing you need is readily at hand, not too neatly stored away.

Above all else, a rural retreat is a place of peace and quiet, somewhere from which you can hear neither the roar of the road traffic nor the roar of the rest of the family. If needs must, you could even colonize the garden shed, clearing out or moving to one side the tools, pots, and seed trays. Sheds can make excellent retreats, and are as close to a custom-built garden office as most of us will ever come. The walk to the shed from the house, even if it is only a few yards long and takes just a few seconds, is the perfect opportunity to change gear mentally and to leave all domestic considerations behind. The shed is psychologically, if not in actuality, well away from it all.

There is a childish temptation to hang a little "Keep Out" sign on the door of a shed retreat, because it will soon become a fiercely guarded private space. And if all you do there is daydream or listen to the radio, who's to know or to criticize? You are in the thick of your own little patch of nature, and you can slow down to its pace and its concerns. Then, watching the blackbirds building their nest, or an ant colony sending its soldiers off on patrol, may provide just the inspiration you have been longing for.

An irresistible corner retreat in a Mediterranean cottage. The cool blues

of the decoration take the heat out of the day and make it an inviting

spot for reading and resting.

And so to an afternoon snooze in the bedroom after an exhausting morning's daydreaming and a bite of lunch. An antique Portuguese iron bed is dressed with lace-trimmed pillows and a floral quilt. The family cat, ever the one to show the way to an easy life, finds no problem in relaxing here.

OUTDOOR LIVING

Room to breathe, room to think

In the fresh air of a room outside

WHEN YOU WALK out into a garden in warm weather, a sense of calm immediately descends. Perhaps there's a breeze, birdsong, perfume from flowers and herbs – enough to distract the senses and the mind and ease the pressures of the day. Outdoor spaces, be they acres of landscaped garden or tiny patios with a few plant pots, can be rooms for living and lounging in, where nature does the decorating with her perfect eye for color and shape.

The key to devising an outdoor room is to approach it in the same way as you would the interior of the home. The sky and the arching shrubs and trees are the ceiling; the grass, stone, brick, or decking is the floor; and the fences and hedges are the walls. The vistas beyond the garden are the views through the windows. Considered in this way, the positioning of furniture and decorative features, and the arrangements and colors of plants, begin to make more sense and seem easier to tackle.

Then there are all the wonderful natural extras that come into play in exterior decoration: the direction and intensity of light and the shadows it creates; the perfume of herbs and flowers; and water, which reflects light and color like an outdoor mirror and introduces sounds. An outdoor space is really a decorator's dream – who needs pictures and prints when real birds and butterflies visit the "room?"

LEFT *This perfect outdoor "room," with its lovely color scheme of pinks, reds, purples, and whites, which has "walls" of tree foliage and a view across farmland. A deck is suspended over a pond, under the shade of a tree.*

RIGHT *A decorative feature in the corner of the "room," incorporating purple clematis and salvias.*

Eating outside is inherently romantic, so it is not difficult to create a table setting that looks special. A plain or patterned cloth draping down into the grass, a simple bowl of flowers, and glasses that reflect the sunlight make the table enticing. Its position – under a tree or next to a flower border, perhaps – is just as important.

Old earthenware flower pots, wooden plant trays, sculptural garden implements: the constituents of the potting shed have an earthiness that is as decorative as it is practical. The look may be old and mucky, but this is where new life begins, whether it is a mass of fragile seedlings potted up or a few bulbs rooting in water containers.

We assume that a country garden will incorporate a vegetable patch, fruit trees growing among the flowers, or a few chickens pecking around in the dirt. After all, what better

decoration could the country kitchen acquire than bowls and baskets of produce freshly picked from the garden and ready for the pot?

Even the most modest garden looks incredibly glamorous when candlelit after dark. An ailing shrub that might not bear close scrutiny in daylight will become a mystical silhouette in the flickering light of a candle. Garden lighting can be used for meals outside, to light the way to the front door, or to create an engaging view from a window.

THE VERANDA, DECK, AND PATIO

The contemporary country home is devoted to the blurring of the boundaries between its interior life and the natural environment outside its walls. The veranda, deck, or patio is situated at just this juncture between the two, representing the best of both worlds and acting as their link. Here, flowers and foliage literally overlap with the man-made architecture and decorations of the house, becoming inseparable. Moss grows up between the bricks of the patio floor; clematis climbs over the banisters of the veranda; and the space is inhabited by greater numbers of insects than of humans.

A veranda is currently seen as a most desirable accoutrement to a house, a decorative and fashionable living space, but its origins are much more functional. The word derives from the Hindi *varanda*, an architectural feature consisting of a roofed gallery extending along the

LEFT *A beautiful wooden veranda running along the side of a country house is painted to harmonize with the surrounding gardens: the floor is a dark olive green, the house wall a sunny yellow, and the woodwork a pale leaf green, which looks lovely with the garden's foliage and purple alliums.*

RIGHT *A different view of the same veranda shows a wooden table set with a delicious seafood lunch. At the far end, the veranda gives onto a patio at the back of the house.*

front, and sometimes around the sides, of a building, for protection from the sun or the rain. As far back as the fifth century, Hindu temples were designed with stone verandas extending all around the outside walls in sweeping curves, acting as airy walkways that kept the elements away from the worshippers.

A veranda is equally valuable today in a hot climate, as it fulfills a dual function: providing a shaded sitting-out area and protecting the walls and windows of the house from direct, fierce sunlight which would heat up the interior like an oven. As world climates warm up generally, and living habits change correspondingly, verandas are now found in areas of more

Three views of a tiny patio garden. Though in a city, it is a country garden in spirit, managing to do a little bit of everything and still look good.

LEFT *Most of its color and foliage come from plantings of vegetables, herbs, and salad plants, many restricted to a collection of terra-cotta pots.*

BELOW LEFT *An improvised brick barbecue is called into service as a plant-stand when not in use for cooking.*

BELOW RIGHT *An old table is disguised with a gingham cloth, and folding chairs are set out for eating. The whole space, including its miniature potting shed, is charming and inviting.*

ABOVE *The colors of autumn bring life to a corner of a patio, where harvested pumpkins and rose-hips are being temporarily stored.*

RIGHT *A modest brick patio outside the back door still has room for a stone bench in the sun, overhung with fragrant, old-fashioned climbing roses.*

temperate climates as well, even if they do have to be abandoned during the winter months. They are no longer merely functional, and their increasing popularity as a feature of new houses results in part from a keen desire to find ways of living in closer harmony with nature.

Larger-scale, traditional verandas are often decorated with an awareness of their historical roots in the East. The furnishings may mix authentic Indian pieces, colonial-style canework, and paisley shawls to defend against an evening chill. The balustrades and supporting columns have elements of Indian decoration, or small pieces of latticework, now made of wood rather than stone, that hang down from the roof gables.

In many American houses, a veranda running across the full width of the house forms the front porch. Furnished with a cushioned swing-seat or wicker rockers, it provides the perfect spot for enjoying a warm summer's evening. At the back of the house, the veranda may translate into a deck, a wooden platform that extends directly out from the house. The natural wood of a deck makes it appropriate to country houses, especially those located in woodland. It is also ideal in situations where the ground is uneven or the house is built on a hillside. Here the deck will be supported on stilts and may be built at more than one level of the slope. For months at a stretch, life is lived on the deck or the front porch, to such an extent that the interior living room is almost irrelevant – the whole family is outside.

Another traditional sitting-out area is the patio, a hard-floored living space with no roof or other protection from the elements. It is also called a terrace, but the word patio is the name that holds the key to its history. Patio is a Spanish word meaning an inner court open to the sky. Southern Spanish architecture is characterized by patios, and is dependent on Moorish styles, introduced during the 500 years of Arab occupation of the region around Andalusia. Moorish houses and palaces were designed around square courtyards with open loggias on all four sides so that breezes could blow through to cool the interiors. The Moorish courtyard was as much a room as any of the interior spaces of the building.

Today's country home patios, courtyards, and decks are more modest in scale and less formal in design, but they nevertheless adopt the same idea of an exterior living room. The idea of using the garden as a living area is increasingly fashionable, with as much attention now paid to the decoration of the hard surfaces of a garden as to its planting.

The patio is where a table might well be positioned for meals outside or for entertaining and where a comfortable garden chair of wicker or canvas might be set out for sitting and reading or cogitating. The patio is

often attached to the house, within easy access of the inside, so that food and tableware and the like can be brought in and out, and everybody can move comfortably between the two spaces.

Certainly, the patio is now the area of the home where the business of relaxing meets the business of working in the garden. Often it is part living room, part pantry, and part potting shed – a place to sit with a glass of wine, to store garden produce, and to grow seedlings or nurture plants that need special care and sheltered conditions. It is usually paved with stone, brick, or pebbles, an informal space which, in true country home style, makes few demands and is casually pretty to look at.

In large gardens there is often the opportunity for more than one patio, and perhaps for a series of sitting-out areas linked by paths meandering through the lawns and flower-beds. The patios can be positioned to catch the sun – or the shade – at different times of the day, or to take in particularly attractive views of the garden or the surrounding landscape. Alternatively, one patio may be designed for

RIGHT *On this deep wooden veranda overlooking a lake, the furniture, although new, suggests the British home in India in the 1920s. There is even a croquet set ready for a languid after-lunch game.*

BELOW *Breakfast on the patio as we imagine it in our most romantic dreams, complete with lace tablecloth, spongeware pitchers and a tin coffeepot. To complete the fantasy, the patio is accessed through French doors from the bedroom.*

entertaining and eating outside, another for quiet reading or for working out-of-doors.

And if you are stuck in town dreaming of the country, it is still possible to create something of the same atmosphere. A small patio garden with screening walls or hedging can be made to look like a little patch of the country in the middle of a city. You may have only a balcony or a fire escape, up which roses and romance can climb, but it is still outside living and sitting space, where pots of flowers can balance and birds can visit.

Two perspectives of a covered deck, raised above the undergrowth in woodland and overlooking a chain of trout ponds. Though similar in style to a veranda, it has been built away from the house for peace and seclusion – and as a prelude to a little fishing.

THE COUNTRY GARDEN

It is almost impossible to picture a country home without thinking of its garden – the two are so intimately connected in our imaginations. What that garden actually looks like, though, is inextricably linked with its location, and with the climate and indigenous plants at the gardener's disposal. A Mediterranean garden, for example, may be no more than a courtyard, with plants – those that can survive the heat, that is – restricted to containers; while an American rural garden may be an extensive, open arrangement of shrubs and trees giving directly onto fields or woodland.

The chocolate-box vision of an old-fashioned cottage garden, in which scented roses tumble around the door and hollyhocks stand proud above a disordered mass of flowering plants, is a strong image. It has little basis in reality, as the typical cottage garden a century or so ago was more likely to be a tiny patch of mud from which the cottager would attempt to eke out a crop of root vegetables – if he was lucky enough to have rights to the land and be able to afford the seed. The romanticized cottage garden style we know and love began to take hold in the late nineteenth century, promulgated by, among others, watercolorists, who created a highly popular genre of paintings depicting a fictitious, sanitized version of rural poverty. In such paintings, children dressed in crisp linens and little bonnets played among the flowers in idealized garden landscapes, and happy housewives paused at the wooden garden gate with a basket of shiny, clean hens' eggs. The reality of these people's lives was totally different and was not one that middle-class Victorians would have liked to see depicted on the walls of their parlors.

Nevertheless, there is no denying that the cottage garden style, which became established by the early decades of the twentieth century, is extremely endearing. Its seemingly random mixture of herbaceous plants, self-seeded and springing into glorious flower spontaneously, is gentle and relaxing, encapsulating all the informality we desire in country living. Perhaps what appeals above all is the lack of competition between the plants, the apparent democracy of it all in which no plant is dominant but each has its own claim to put on a show.

In the garden, as in the interior of the home, an informal, not too ordered look is paradoxically much more difficult to achieve than something stricter. Exercising a *laissez-faire* control over plants is a skill that comes only with considerable gardening experience and a great many hours spent in peaceful contemplation of the garden. There is just a hair's breadth between the pleasing jumble of cottage garden style and a

Candlelight in the garden is always enchanting. It probably has something to do with movement – the flickering of the flames corresponding to the rustling of leaves. Live, burning flames, rather than electric lights, have the added advantage of keeping away mosquitoes and other unwelcome evening insect life, particularly if the candle wax is treated with an aromatic deterrent. There are many ways of using candlelight in the garden, as these photographs show – anything from a simple, suspended jar to a magnificent candelabra.

total mess of unhappy-looking plants. That said, what could be lovelier in summer than the colorful, fragrant flowers of columbines, daisies, campanulas, and peonies, with honeysuckle clambering out of the fray and up the walls?

Another characteristic of the country garden is that it harmonizes gently with the surrounding landscape, so that the one flows into the other. It is part of the desire for a natural transition, a breaking down of boundaries, between the interior of the house, the casually contrived garden, and the countryside beyond. Unlike town gardens, where high walls and hedging plants are used to block out unattractive urban surroundings, country gardens encourage vistas to the fields and woods, capitalizing on space and openness. A low hedge, wall, or ditch or even just the contrast between mown and unmown grass may be the only demarcation of the territory of the garden.

Country gardens are generally larger in area than those in town and therefore provide more scope for planting. There is likely to be plenty of room for flower borders, lawn, trees, shrubberies, a pond perhaps, and, importantly, a kitchen garden to produce fresh vegetables, fruits, and herbs for the country kitchen cook. For many country dwellers, the kitchen garden is an essential element of the rural dream, part of a desire to become self-sufficient in food, or at least to take a step in that direction. There is no denying that the creation of a vegetable garden requires thought and hard work, but the rewards are well worth the effort. Once you have tasted fresh vegetables picked from the garden minutes before they go into the pan, there is no return to the blandness of supermarket varieties. And once you have

LEFT *Vegetables and herbs – including fava beans, spinach, and chives – are mixed together in a tiny kitchen garden plot, which is edged with box.*

BELOW *A larger and more conventional vegetable plot is planted up in rows of the same crop, each alternating with a row of a different variety of lettuce.*

smelled the extraordinary perfume of a ripe tomato plucked straight from the vine, you are captivated to the extent that you will water the tomato plants religiously every evening.

The growing of produce can be a formal affair, involving strict rows of plants or canes, or it can be absorbed into the rest of the planting scheme. In recent years, it has become fashionable to mix borders so that vegetables and herbs pop up quite happily in between more conventional flowers and shrubs. Fruit trees have long been incorporated into the overall design of a cottage garden – apples, pears, cherries, and plums, in particular, providing blossoms and fruits that are as decorative as they are functional. Many herbs, fruits, vegetables, and salad plants are, in any case, attractive, some having impressive foliage, others featuring striking flowers. Purple sprouting broccoli has wonderful gray-green and mauve foliage, carrot leaves are pretty little ferns, beets have dark red, broad leaves. The fernlike foliage of asparagus is much loved by flower arrangers. Rhubarb has its characteristic red stems and huge, architectural

BELOW LEFT *Wild foxgloves traditionally self-seed wherever they choose, attracting bees on their first, early-summer forays for nectar.*

foliage, while raspberries and loganberries make lovely hedging plants, rambling along with white flowers and then red ripening fruits.

If there really isn't enough space for a substantial fruit and vegetable garden, or if you are, in fact, living in town and dreaming of country garden style, the answer may lie with a herb garden. Whether it is for culinary or medicinal use, you do not need vast quantities, and the herb patch can occupy a very small area. Within that, though, plants of different heights and with a variety of foliage, flowers, and perfumes can be selected. Herb gardens are irresistible, with their little shrubby thymes at the front, purple pompoms of chives behind, and tarragons and angelicas towering at the back. And if the colors of the herbs' flowers seem a little subdued – predominantly purples and whites – there is nothing like the addition of brilliant orange pot marigolds to lift the appeal of the herb palette.

So, however big or small, and wherever it is, the country garden is a bustling tangle of trees, flowers, bushes, and edible plants in which

BELOW CENTER *Geese are used as ecologically sound lawnmowers in this country garden, bright with a number of poppy cultivars in mid-summer.*

BELOW RIGHT *A perfect place in which to hide away and read, concealed among the flowers and ferns of a wild country garden.*

branches and scents are interwoven. It is the perfect place in which to sit out and relax, in a confortable chair hidden beneath overhanging branches of a tree or on a bench positioned at a point where the view of the garden is at its best. The garden is a refuge, but it is not a retreat in the same way as some interior spaces of the home are. This is a highly sociable place where you are never alone, but rather surrounded by many other animal species. Some are small mammals – squirrels, chipmunks, and an assortment of different bird species – or you may have your own domestic garden roamers, such as hens or geese, and family pets such as a cat or dog. But the real inhabitants of the garden, those to whom it truly belongs and who keep the soil aerated and the flowers pollinated, are the insects. Even on the quietest day, there remain the sounds of them going about their daily lives. It is astonishing, for example, how loud the noise of a single wasp chewing at a wooden fence is on a still summer's evening.

It is equally satisfying to be sociable with members of our own species. Meals eaten outside with friends or family are memorable, and always seem to be recalled as long, languid, and relaxed. In the garden there is no need to sit up straight and observe all the formalities, and awkward silences can't develop when there is the sound of nature all around. Children can scatter crumbs and lean back in their chairs without reproach, and a fly in your soup is just par for the course. If the weather behaves, the setting outside is automatically perfect.

Even a rickety old trestle table is charming in the garden, with a crisp gingham cloth thrown over it and some plain earthenware plates and café tumblers. For special occasions, the table can be imaginatively dressed, with colorful tableware and glasses, and pitchers of flowers picked from the garden. The natural surroundings of the outdoor "room" are an inspiration for its colors and decorations. Yellow table linen may be prompted by a wall of climbing golden roses, for example, while a striking blue and white table setting would be the obvious choice for a meal eaten under the lilac trees.

On a sunny day, tree branches or a vine-covered pergola provides the most wonderful dappled shade, a great natural advantage of the outdoor "room." After dark, it can become a place of mystery and romance, lit by votives in lanterns hanging from the trees and by floating candles in wide bowls of water, mixed with scented flowers or blossom.

Many of the best gardens succeed because they are able to create a sense of mystery and surprise. Paths that are winding, rather than straight, can lead the way through flower-beds, or link one garden "room" with another. They also make a garden seem much larger, as the eye is taken on a little tour rather than being dragged straight to the far end. Special plants, or decorative features such as furniture or sculpture, placed on bends in the pathways, will particularly catch the eye. The paths may be of old brick with mosses and small plants growing

LEFT *Lunch out on the lawn couldn't be more perfect than in this setting of dappled light under the arching branches of trees, near enough to the house to dash in for a missing dish and to enjoy the arrangement of flowers in pots on the patio.*

BELOW *A designer has been working outdoors in summer at this simple trestle table, positioned in such a way that it is shaded from direct sun and from winds.*

between, of woodblocks or railroad sleepers, of gravel, pebbles, or grass. There could be a pattern worked into the hard surfacing, such as a pebble mosaic or choice large stones, or you could even consider a miniature maze made up of lines of bricks on the ground.

Garden sculpture takes many different forms. Traditional stone statues or classical urns, planted with flowers or standing alone, look totally natural emerging from the undergrowth, particularly if they are encrusted with lichen or wound around with ivy. A garden can become a marvelous outdoor gallery for contemporary sculpture and will accommodate much larger pieces than most interiors. Dense foliage makes a good backdrop for curious relics of farm implements or machinery – rusty and twisted old metal can look altogether more exotic in such a setting. Grotesque masks on garden walls, anthropomorphic fountains, incongruous designs, or unexpected materials can all contribute elements of surprise or humor which make the garden individualistic and interesting.

Water features and ponds add a lot to the country-style garden, evoking images of free-flowing streams. However large or small the expanse of water, it is always soothing, reflecting the light and the plants, enhancing the look of the garden. In most gardens, whatever their size, space can be found for a water feature of some sort. A fountain introduces the sound of running water and looks especially effective if the water flows over a bed of pebbles, while a pond will bring in more wildlife, such as fish, frogs, and dragonflies, and enable the gardener to use a whole new range of plants, including water lilies and wild irises.

Children adore ponds, but they also love a secret treehouse, however modest, or a rope ladder or swing suspended from a sturdy tree. Magical outdoor play areas deliver experiences that we remember all our lives.

RIGHT *Accessed via duckboards across the marshy edge of a lake, this contemporary boathouse offers a place to sit and enjoy privileged peace and privacy.*

BELOW *A cabin with a tower presides over a serious fruit and vegetable garden on one side, and undulating farmland on the other. Rhubarb is ingeniously planted in an old metal trash can to keep the unruly plant neatly contained.*

THE GARDEN SHED

Not long ago, the garden shed was regarded as an unattractive necessity that was best kept out of sight. Gardeners would go to great lengths to site it in the most unobtrusive corner of the garden – behind trees or shrubs or at the side of the house – and would then take pains to grow climbers across the roof to try to make it even less visible.

In recent years, however, the shed's image has been lifted – so much so that it is now seen as a highly desirable asset. This is in part because designers have been giving sheds something of a makeover, and now they

A shed used as a retreat is provided with a pair of large windows and a garden bench. It is meant to be seen, not hidden, so it is painted bright blue.

feature as garden follies, attractive and amusing little structures, of greater significance in the landscape than somewhere simply to store tools. There is now a whole new genre of shed architecture, with many people commissioning their own customized designs.

Sheds have historically been the butt of comedians' jokes, characterized as the only place to which the disgruntled male of the household could escape to read his newspaper uninterrupted. Peace and quiet were found at the bottom of the garden, away from family life. However, attitudes to sheds soon began to change. Many people found shed escapism a compelling option, and sheds began to acquire a status as legitimate

The garden shed has here become the garden shop, from which its owners sell herbs, plants, baskets, and garden paraphernalia.

retreats (see Chapter Four). Like grown-up doll houses, many have become rooms where adults go to play. With space in many homes at a premium, more and more sheds have been emptied, given a new lick of paint, and provided with a heater. Some have running water, coffee-making facilities, day-beds, pictures on the walls, and cushions on the chairs. They are almost like second homes.

Even when they are still being used for potting, sheds are more attractive than they were and are now allowed to be on public view. In the age of nurseries and gardening shortcuts, perhaps there is a desire to show off the fact that the gardener is doing his or her own propagation and potting out, so the donkey-work becomes part of the garden display. Images of seedling trays, flower specimens in terra-cotta pots, wheelbarrows full of bulbs and corms, and trugs of cut flowers are part of our nostalgia for imagined times past. These are as intrinsic to country gardens as collections of glazed earthenware are to country kitchens.

The wholly functional garden shed, used exclusively as a store for tools and other garden and household pieces, also looks good in the country garden, as it denotes an honest day's work. A pile of chopped logs or a watering can at the ready shows that country living is underway for real. An old-fashioned garden scythe or bicycle without gears indicates that the owner of the garden is fit and active and not ashamed of hard work. Whereas once these features would be embarrassing evidence of a lack of staff to undertake life's more mundane tasks, they are now a cause for celebration that a simpler way of life has been rediscovered.

LEFT ABOVE *Hand-woven willow trays are lined with newspaper and labeled to receive various crops from the garden.*

LEFT BELOW *The most basic shed structure, with its corrugated iron roof, takes on a simple beauty nevertheless. Antique garden and farm implements outside the shed are attractive pieces, and a couple of hanging baskets filled with summer bedding plants add color.*

*Spring is in the air and the magnolia is
in bloom, so why stay indoors? Come
outside and live in the garden. An
irresistible table is laid with linen so fine
it looks like voile and with colored
glassware that picks up the first rays of
warm sunshine.*

AUTHOR'S ACKNOWLEDGMENTS

I would like to thank all at Country Living magazine who advised and commented on the book, and Susanna van Langenberg and her staff at The National Magazine Company picture library, who facilitated the selection of the photographs.

Many thanks go to the Collins & Brown team: in particular to Gillian Haslam, project editor, for her calm manner and for her management of all the complexities of putting the book together; to Christine Wood, for her attractive and accessible design of the book; and to Alison Wormleighton, for applying her thorough copy editor's eye to my text.

As ever, friends and relations sustained me, and to them my love and thanks.

PHOTOGRAPHIC ACKNOWLEDGMENTS

Michael Arnaud 30 (bottom)
Jan Baldwin 35, 112 (top left), 144 (bottom right), 165 (top)
Tim Beddow 15 (bottom right), 23, 43, 44, 90, 114 (top right)
Mark Bolton 115 (top left)
Henry Bourne 16 (top left), 118
Simon Brown 30 (top)
Tim Clinch 34 (bottom), 38, 93
Charlie Colmer 7, 14 (top right), 15 (top left), 47 (bottom left), 49 (bottom left and right), 52, 53, 59, 62, 65, 66, 73, 78 (bottom right), 79 (bottom right), 81 (bottom right), 97, 98, 117, 125, 128, 141, 169, 170 (bottom), 173
Harry Cory-Wright 16 (bottom right)
Steve Dalton 105
Christopher Drake 15 (top right, bottom left), 29, 34 (top), 37, 47 (bottom right), 78 (top right), 79 (bottom left), 81 (bottom left), 106, 113 (top left and right), 122, 123 (left and right), 135 (right)
Melanie Eclare 162 (right)
Craig Fordham 121 (right)
Kate Gadsby 142, 143
Jane Gifford 146 (bottom right)
John Glover 160
Huntley Hedworth 14 (bottom right), 16 (top right), 17 (top right, bottom left), 22, 27, 39, 46 (bottom left and right), 47 (top right), 48 (top left), 49 (top left and right), 57, 58, 61 (right), 69, 75, 76, 77, 80 (bottom left and right), 81 (top left), 85 (top and bottom), 92, 96 (left), 104 (left and right), 112 (top right), 116, 131 (bottom), 145 (top left)
Jacqui Hurst 146 (top right), 161, 162 (left), 163 (right)
Sandra Lane 128
Tom Leighton 17 (top left), 102, 103 (bottom), 137
Mark Luscombe-White 74, 108, 109, 110, 111, 140

Jill Mead 146 (top left)
James Merrell 10, 11, 13, 16 (bottom left), 20, 24, 28, 42, 46 (top left), 47 (top left), 48 (top right, bottom left and right), 55, 56, 63, 70, 71, 78 (top left) 80 (top left and right), 81 (top right), 82, 83, 91, 94, 95, 96 (right), 100, 101, 112 (bottom left and right), 114 (top left and bottom left), 115 (bottom right), 120, 124, 130, 131 (top), 153, 165 (bottom)
Clay Perry 36
Nick Pope 154
Spike Powell 150, 151 (left and right)
Alex Ramsey 2, 8, 18, 46 (top right), 68, 126, 134, 156, 157, 166, 167
Trevor Richards 61 (left)
Kim Sayer 1
Heini Schneebeli 152
William Shaw 146 (bottom left)
Ron Sutherland 14 top left), 21, 78 (bottom left), 79 (top left), 89, 127
Pia Tryde 5, 9, 12, 19, 26, 31, 40, 50, 113 (bottom right), 114 (bottom right), 132, 133, 144 (top left and right, bottom left), 145 (top right, bottom left and right), 147, 155, 150 (top left, bottom right), 158, 178 (top left, bottom right), 170 (top)
Simon Upton 88, 113 (bottom left), 115 (top right, bottom left), 121 (left), 138
Rodney Weidland 148, 149
Peter Woloszynski 14 (bottom left), 17 (bottom right), 79 (top right), 86, 99, 103 (top)
Ling Wong 135 (left), 168

Styling by **Hester Page, Ben Kendrick, Pippa Rimmer, Gabi Tubbs** and **Margaret Caselton**.